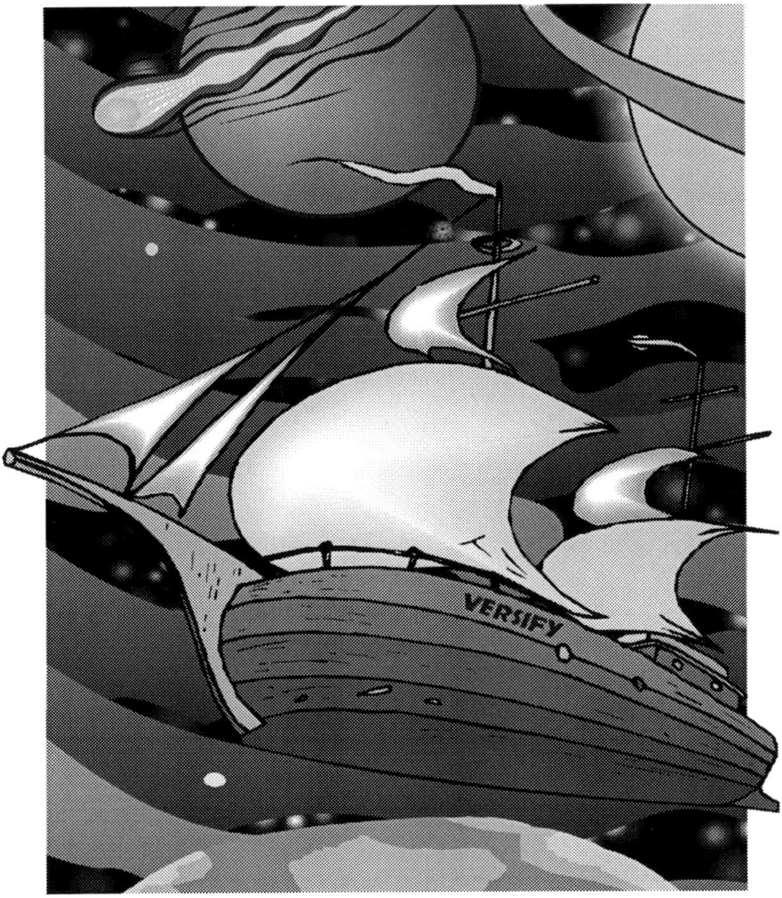

POETIC VOYAGES EAST LONDON

Edited by Steve Twelvetree

First published in Great Britain in 2002 by
YOUNG WRITERS
Remus House,
Coltsfoot Drive,
Peterborough, PE2 9JX
Telephone (01733) 890066

HB ISBN 0 75433 470 8
SB ISBN 0 75433 471 6

FOREWORD

Young Writers was established in 1991 with the aim to promote creative writing in children, to make reading and writing poetry fun.

This year once again, proved to be a tremendous success with over 88,000 entries received nationwide.

The Poetic Voyages competition has shown us the high standard of work and effort that children are capable of today. It is a reflection of the teaching skills in schools, the enthusiasm and creativity they have injected into their pupils shines clearly within this anthology.

The task of selecting poems was therefore a difficult one but nevertheless, an enjoyable experience. We hope you are as pleased with the final selection in *Poetic Voyages East London* as we are.

CONTENTS

The Poems

I Had A Kitten Long Ago

I had a kitten long ago but
Then he passed away
I cried and cried
I wish he hadn't died
By being run over by a taxi driver.
He was only one year old and was very young for his age,
He died straight away as he was hit
All I got from the vets was his collar
To remember him forever.
I don't think he's with the Devil,
I know he's in Heaven
Looking down at his house every night.
I pray to God to look over him and I missed him the most in my family
I had a big broken heart.

April McDonald (10)
Barclay Junior School

Scary Plane

Deep between every road and lane there runs a road called Scary Plane
It is a road that nobody has seen
You only know it because it's mean,
It is so mean you wouldn't be keen to go there
But one day a man of forty whose name was Alfred Courtney
Went down every road
And down every lane and found Scary Plane
And at once he changed his mode.
He got his video camcorder out filming a dog on a log
Suddenly the camera was knocked out of his hand
And that was the end of Alfred Courtney and his cam.

Jack Sim (10)
Barclay Junior School

SUSPENDED

As I looked at the door of my house
I saw the teacher standing there.
I remembered
It ain't a Saturday,
It ain't a holiday,
Then my parent-carer said
'How could I have forgotten that?'
I had given her an extra key.
All this time she was talking and
She never let her eyes off work.
Then I accidentally burped in front of Miss Kurt,
Then she suspended me and reminded me
At school Ryu was making a fool out of Sue
And everyone thought it was cool
Then my teacher said
'It ain't a Saturday,
It ain't a holiday,
So if you stay away
You'll get thrown away.'

Fungai Phanuel Marange (10)
Barclay Junior School

MY JOURNEY TO THE SEA

My journey to the sea
Took place when I hurt my knee
The sea is like a really big blue blanket
Until my mother went and drank it.

This is how the story went
When the water pipe got bent
My mum felt very thirsty
A woman got livid, her name was Kirsty.

Then my mum looked at the sea
With those big eyes she scared me
She drank the sea all up
And she thought Kirsty was a chocolate cup.

My mum grew one hundred feet tall
And we all looked so, so small
My mum ate Kirsty
Then she wasn't thirsty.

Vijay Parmar (9)
Barclay Junior School

THE BATTLE OF PERSEUS AND MEDUSA

Getting near, getting near
Getting near onward
Into the dark cave
Went Perseus.

Forward went Perseus
'Don't stop!' He said
'Keep going!' He said
The more near he got.

Darkness to the right of him,
Darkness to the left of him,
Darkness to the front of him,
As he went on.

Bang!
Through the dark cave
Shattered the dark ranks
Capture the head - all thanks
To Perseus
He did what he had to do.

Andrew Lee (9)
Barclay Junior School

Spring

Daffodils are popping up
Children playing in their gardens.

Violets pushing through the ground
Snow is going and grass is growing.

New born lambs
Farmers sowing seeds.

Cattle begin to graze
The winter laze is over.

The sun is beginning to shine
Clouds begin to fade.

Nights are shorter
Days are longer.

Spring is here
Winter's gone
But now I think spring is going
And summer's coming.

Rachel Harris (10)
Barclay Junior School

A Day In The Life Of Our Big Brother

Our big brother wakes up
Shouts at me,
Has breakfast,
And still moans at me.

Our big brother comes home from school
Has a groan,
Watches TV,
Does his homework,
And moans at me.

Our big brother wakes up
Plays on his Playstation,
Gets in trouble,
And still moans at me.

Shamsa Mahmood (8) & Gabrielle Downer (9)
Barclay Junior School

Zoo Friends

First we step out the door
We arrive at the zoo gates
Over there will be all our mates.

Now we will go and see the anteater
With his pink pants
He will see some little black creatures
They are called ants.

Baboon is the tough guy
All black and brown
When he is really happy
He will jump up and down.

Wild cats are running about all around the zoo
They can hear really well
Might just hear a cow moo.

Now it's time to go home
It's been a great day
We want to eat our dinner
We will come another day.

Kiyaan Ramjan (8)
Barclay Junior School

Going Out To Play

Away, away, I'm going out to play and shan't be back until tea
So please don't worry about me.
I'll be with my friends at the cinema,
Then maybe we'll go to the park
If you want to know my friends' names
They are Santanah, Sarah and Mark.
Please, please don't worry
I promise I'll be back before dark
I don't know what the fuss is
I'm only going to the park.
I'll probably need some money
About ten pounds please
And yes, yes, yes I promise
I won't spend it all on sweets.
I'll also need some bus fare
Well that's about it.
Back soon Mummy, Daddy
Goodbye, adios and goodnight.

Michaela Marius (10)
Barclay Junior School

The Lights Of London

In London the lights are flashing
Twinkle, twinkle, twinkle.
Everyone thinks the lights are clashing
Twinkle, twinkle, twinkle.

If you're in a shop the lights will be flashing
Twinkle, twinkle, twinkle.
All around you, are dashing men
Twinkle, twinkle, twinkle.

All the people are sad now
Sad, sad, sad.
Because the lights have been turned off now
Sad, sad, sad.

Hannah Amartey (9)
Barclay Junior School

ANIMALS

There are many animals
Big or small
All different sizes,
Short and tall.

All animals will never be
All the same
Some are wild
And some are tame.

I'd keep pets of any sort,
Wild or a house pet,
Or if it came from a farm
Keeping either I won't regret.

Puppies have such little eyes
And cats have such tiny paws,
And foxes have such bushy tails
And lions have such enormous claws.

I think animals
Are really cool
I don't love one animal
I love them all!

Hayley Delew (10)
Barclay Junior School

DANIEL'S POEMS

I went to Abbot's Park
Until it got very dark.

I was mopping the floor
And then I heard a knock at the door.

I was playing on my drum
And then I had to go out with my mum.

I like jam
But I don't eat ham.

I like playing my Nintendo 64
But I prefer to draw.

I like winter
But I prefer the summer.

I was playing my Playstation
But then I had to go to the petrol station.

I like drawing
But sometimes it gets boring.

I was hitting the wall with a broom,
Then my mum told me to go to my room.

In south, east England I was born and raised,
At the park is where I spend most of my days.

Daniel Small (8)
Barclay Junior School

HEADLESS RIDING HOOD

In a horrible cottage
She will die if she's rotted
The headless beast's life will never end
She's hunting . . . just hunting . . . to end your life!

She will transform in the end
Then she will be your best friend
But she's kidding to be the best friend
She's hunting . . . just hunting . . . to end your life!

Faizal Patel (8)
Barclay Junior School

MY LITTLE FLOWER

From just a seed I watch you grow
What you will be I am longing to know
I water you daily until to my surprise
Tiny leaves start to reach the skies
Then a flower reaches so high
My little flower
How I love you so I had so much fun to watch you grow.

As the autumn comes along
I watch your song fade away
And then the earth begins to say
Your time has come
Your petals have fell
You're getting old
Your owners can tell
Before you go I must say you have lived a life of fun and play
As you go your roots will stay they all love you so be on your way.

And in the summer to my surprise
Your tiny shoots begin to rise
And as the seasons come and go
I know your roots they will re-grow.

Tammy Gittins (10)
Barclay Junior School

THE SUN AND THE MOON

The sun is a gem
Stuck in the sky.
It is a medal
Shouting with joy.

The sun is a lemon
Shooting out sour drops.

The sun is a new born chick
Scratching for tiny grains.

It is a fireball
Burning with lava
Across the world.

The sun is an orange
Till the sun falls down
And it is night again.

The moon is a white sparkling diamond
On a ring worn by a pretty bride.

The moon is a rabbit's tail
As soft as a baby's bottom.

The moon is a dove
Flying across the navy blue sky
Till the last stroke strikes midnight.

Sara Malek (10)
Barclay Junior School

THE TEACHER WHO HATES CHILDREN

The teacher writes with a big chalk,
And she shouts out no one can talk
She waits for you to fight or swear then
She's waiting . . . just waiting . . . to give you a detention!

The teacher hates ugly, dirty, hideous kids
She puts them in pots with a lid
But behind her she's holding a tracking sheet
And she's waiting . . . just waiting . . . to give you a detention!

Angela Khokhar (9) & Tayyaba Khanam Rafi (8)
Barclay Junior School

JOURNEY TO THE PLANETS

10, 9, 8, 7, 6, 5,
Computers buzzing - circuit's alive
4, 3, 2, 1, zero fire,
Power courses through every wire,
The shining spaceship lifts into space
Looking like a silver mace.

The moon a silver glistering sphere
Grows bigger as the spaceship gets near,
Retros fire, prepare to land
Touchdown moon on light grey sand,
Refuel by means of lunar cars,
Blast off again to objective Mars.

A dusty, red-green lifeless globe,
Appears in the porthole of the probe,
This is Mars, red planet of mystery
Which has influenced mankind since prehistory,
We orbit once, then pass Mars by,
And fly into the starlit sky.

Venus glowing, sparkling bright,
Letting out an awesome light,
We study the cloud filled dome,
Then change our course and head for home.

M Hussain Patel (9)
Barclay Junior School

(You) I Will See You

When I look in the sky (I see you),
You make me lie, you make me cry (I see you),
When you look at me (I see you),
You're always in my thoughts.

My eyes are like windows I see straight through them,
(I see you)
I can see you,
I will see you,
I want to see you,
I should see you.

One day up there in Heaven (I will see you)
Would you look after me and make sure I am safe in your chamber?
You have got the key, look after my family and also you would see me!

Sara Campbell (11)
Barclay Junior School

Acrostic Poems

W ater is cold
A pples are growing
T rees are green
E at all your dinner
R oses are red.

S ea is cold
P eople are wet
R ed apples are wet
N ettles sting
I ce is cold
N ever be bad
G rowing strawberries.

Dominique Harris (7)
Barclay Junior School

A HAPPY BIRTHDAY TO YOU

H is for being happy when it's my birthday,
A is for all of you and me having a fun time,
P is for party poppers,
P is for playing games on my birthday,
Y is for you and me eating some food.

B is for balloons on my birthday
I is for interesting games,
R is for racing for the games,
T is for a tea game,
H is for having a fun time on my birthday
D is for delicious food
A is for mini apple pies yum, yum
Y is for yummy food.

T is for tasty food
O is for playing the Olympic Games.

Y is for yo-yo for my birthday present
O is for oranges yum, yum
U is for umbrella if it rains on my birthday.

Margam Choudhery (9)
Barclay Junior School

THE SUN

The sun looks like a golden ball,
It smells like a sweaty cold,
It sounds like a black pepper,
It tastes like hot sizzling pepper,
It feels like fluffy cotton wool.
In the morning it's white and grey,
It's shiny and round like a ball.

Gzim Niky (9)
Barclay Junior School

Animal Poem

One little cat sitting
    On the wall
He jumped off to chase
    The ball.

One little bird sitting
    In a tree
Looking as far as he
    Could see.

One big dog chewing
    His bone
He broke his teeth
    On a stone.

One furry rabbit sitting
    In a hutch
But no one could touch!

Zahra Naeem (10)
Barclay Junior School

Bloodthirsty Pirates

The bloodthirsty pirates come on their blood-thirsty pirate ship
They throw someone in the pan and fry them
Throw tins and cans
They are waiting . . .
Just waiting to stab you.
They come on a deserted dark night
What they'll do to you
They are just waiting . . .
Just waiting . . .
To get you.

Aamir Mirza (8) & Sohail Hassan Aziz (9)
Barclay Junior School

My Feelings

I am very good sometimes
But sometimes I'm really sad
Not even a person helps me
Then I definitely go mad.

So it was just then
When I was nineteen years old
It was just time for
Me to get more gold.

My worst feeling was
When my bike was on fire
So I decided to get the
Bike a new tyre.

So it was just then
When I was twenty years old
So I decided to
Have my house sold.

Adnan Bashir (9)
Barclay Junior School

Riddles

I start and stop
The police need one on the sea,
I need a key to start me.
I go really fast,
But I don't last.
More than one passenger can come on me
People don't always use me,
But it would be good for me,
So my battery does not die.

Haroon Arshad (11)
Barclay Junior School

My Bed

In my bed I lay in this stormy weather
And when I look above
I see a lovely feather
And I say to the feather
My bed is warm
It keeps me away from the storm.
Oh! My bed, my lovely bed
Whatever will I do without my bed
When my mummy calls me to go to school
I just keep on sleeping and start to drool.
When I wake up to watch some telly
And on a cookery programme I see some jelly
I run down the stairs to eat some food
And now I notice there is nothing here.
Uh oh! We're moving again
So when I go back upstairs
I want my bed!

Zahra Aziz Shah (9)
Barclay Junior School

Bubblegum

Bubblegum is chewy
Up on the ceiling I see a bit of gum
Bubble up your drink
Baby brother blow some bubbles
Late again for bubbly school
Even my big bubbly brother's late.

Gummy mummy is not awake
Umm I wonder what's for lunch
Mmm nice bubbly cake.

Lucy Christodoulou (8)
Barclay Junior School

The Little Monkey

Families and couples went to the zoo
One little girl crying because she's got the flu.
All the animals making their sounds
And one little monkey swinging, fell to the ground.

All the people laughed, to them it was a joke
But the little monkey hated being laughed at by old folk.
The little monkey angrily walked into his cage
Which rattled with old age.

I wish I was at home with Mum and Dad
This made him think of a plan that made him very glad.
He opened the cage and went out of the zoo
He also saw the girl that had the flu.

He swung from tree to tree and landed at home
When he saw his mum and dad he never felt alone.

Nobelle Wallace (9)
Barclay Junior School

Who Dat Boy?

Who dat boy wid im funny ear,
Wid im curly hair,
And im white bright teet,
Sitten down on im likkle chair?

Who dat boy wid im dark eye,
An im nails as long as can be?
Im staring at me, im staring at me!

Who dat likkle boy? Who dat likkle boy?
Dat likkle boy is me.

Abigail Mills (9)
Barclay Junior School

My Party

My party starts at one p.m.
I wake up here and now I'm ten
I blow balloons and look outside,
Till anybody will arrive.

I see my friend with a prezzie there
Her name is Claire with nice blonde hair,
She knocks on the door, I open it wide,
I see her blue eyes and I move aside.

I say to her 'Why thank you my friend!
It's nice of you to attend'
She loves to eat a nice fruit cake
My mum made one and she baked, baked, baked.

My other friends did arrive,
We went swimming and had a dive,
I will remember this party,
Till the day I have a nice Smartie.

Amina Siddique (10)
Barclay Junior School

The Land Of The Puddley Poo

In the land of the Puddley Poo
The people always chew
They never have fun
Or ever drink rum
What a lovely place to do.

In the land of Puddley Poo
You can eat lots of goo!
They give away a cake
In an oven to bake
And boxes of something to chew.

Manzar Hussain Khan (11)
Barclay Junior School

Two Little Ducks

Two little ducks twaddling along
One called Jane, the other called John
Jane comes to me and says 'Wee wee'
Then John comes over driving his Rover
And he gives Jane a four-leafed clover.
Then they get into the car
But drive into a bar
Luckily, that's OK
Because they didn't have to pay!
The day after that John met a bat
He said 'Hi!'
But the bat said 'Bye'
Then Jane comes along with a Christmas pie
The Christmas pie went in the little bat's eye
And he started to cry
He said 'Bye bye' with a tear in his eye
And that was the end of the day.

Isabella Brinsmead (9)
Barclay Junior School

APADOR

There was a man
His name was Stan
He liked to eat potatoes.
He had a dog
His name was Pog
Who couldn't bark to save us.
One day a man knocked at the door
He sold them tickets to Apador.
They left in a rocket
With food in their pocket
And flew through the stars to the far away planet.
Apador was so hot
Their food started to rot
And Stan and his dog couldn't bear it.
So they said their goodbyes
And took to the skies
And came back down to Earth to cool off.

Miles Cooper (10)
Barclay Junior School

SCHOOL

Today is my first day of school
I don't want to go
I think the teachers will be mean
And make me miss my playtime.
I think the children will be mean and bully me
And put me in the cellar where the rats live
And kick me, hit me and spit at me.
My mum is having to drag me down the road.
I'm at the gates and I think I might like it.

Patrick Camm (10)
Barclay Junior School

Riddles

Sometimes I am fast
Sometimes slow,
But whichever way
I know where to go.

I make you cold,
I make you hot,
Then when you put on your hat
Scarf,
Coat
And gloves
You are steaming like a firing pot
I can make things drop and fall
And go round and round.

rewsnA - ehT dniW.

Cassandra Toussaint (10)
Barclay Junior School

A Day In The Life Of Raichu

Raichu wakes,
Electrocutes itself,
Eats,
Goes in the garden,
Sleeps,
Raichu wakes,
Digs,
Goes under the fence,
Sleeps,
Raichu wakes,
Sleeps.

Ayrton Hall (8)
Barclay Junior School

My Memory On The Beach

Bringing back a memory a long time ago
Of sand between my toes
The smell of sun lotion up my nose
A sudden breeze from the wind
A relaxed sight from the blue sky
Collecting shells from the seashore
Smooth, rough, small, big, white, light, short, tall,
Whirly, swirly, fat, skinny, pointy, sharp
Children laughing, playing games
Ladies sunbathing in the sun
While men are surfing with glee
The night sky hangs over the light sky
The stars twinkle in the sky
The fun is over, time to pack away.

Philippa Michael (9)
Barclay Junior School

Bart's Life

Wakes up,
Has his breakfast,
Goes to school,
Had a detention,
Comes home,
Wakes up,
Has his breakfast,
Goes to his tree house,
Plays computer,
Comes home.

Ahmet Kadri & Sibtain Dar (9)
Barclay Junior School

The Pain

There was a girl, her name was Jane
She lived down Mulberry Lane
And she had a friend called Annabell.

She had a dog she wanted to sell
An ugly man walked up the lane
He looked a bit insane and he was a pain.

He asked 'What's the dog's name?'
'His name is Kane' said Jane
So the man said 'How much is he?'
'He is £50 and 25p.'
'I think I do not want to buy him now' he said
'That man's a pain' said Jane.

'I'll buy the dog' said Jane
'Because you can see him play
And you can see him any day.'

Kimberleigh Armsby (10)
Barclay Junior School

Little Kitty

Kitty comes out every night
Kitty doesn't like the light
She always whines and always twines every night,
She has sharp nails like her teeth
She loves to eat
And her eyes are green as a leaf
Finally Kitty falls asleep
And she cuddles up in her little warm bed
With her little head poking out.

Taiba Ahmed (9)
Barclay Junior School

THE SKY

The sky is so high
I just can't touch it
I see the birds flying by
I feel the breeze which touches my cheek
And it makes me feel tingly inside.

I see the sun come out from behind the clouds,
I see the sun and the sun sees me
Behind a wooden tree.

Now it's night-time
The sky is dark as a black blanket
I see the stars shining brightly
Now it's time for bed
Goodnight sky!

Santanah Cole (9)
Barclay Junior School

POEMS, POEMS

Poems, poems are really fun
All the ideas might come from a bun
Well I don't know
Do you believe the bell at Bow?
They brought a bunny with my money
They have to owe me back
If not I will give them the sack
If you don't believe me go eat a pea
Then you will learn
Try not to burn
Your head
Even when it's time for bed.

Sabrina Mahmood (9)
Barclay Junior School

Star Shapes

A star is a feather
From a dove's wing.

It's a silver yo-yo
Bouncing on its string.

A star is a teardrop
Falling down night's face
It's a milky snowflake
Patterned like lace.

A star is a jewel
In the Queen's crown
It's a hole in the sky
To let angels look down.

Aymen Rabio (9)
Barclay Junior School

The Funfair Playground

In the playground,
Nice and big
When we're playing
We enjoy ourselves,
And have fun.
In the shed
There are droppings.
The trees blow by
As we walk to our lines
The trees are as green as grass,
To make it look like a garden
When people play they have fun
To make it a happy playground.

Sherelle Johnson (9)
Barclay Junior School

A Rocky View That I See

I look out of my window
And I look at the sea.
It's such a lovely view
It's as blue as blue can be.

It reminds me of when I have a bath
All the water's on my pore
Filling me up to the brim
Like the pebbles on the shore.

The mountains are big and rocky
They're dark and blueish grey
They are so hard and still
They will never go away.

The sun shines in the morning
So bright and joyful
The moon shines at night
And the bright stars sparkle.

I'm going downstairs
And out the front door
I love to see this view
More and more and more.

There are lots of creatures in the water
Like dolphins, whales and fish
Why do they use the poor things
To appease man's culinary wish?

The moon is up
My bed is calling me
I'm going back inside
For a lovely cup of tea!

Malisha Lindo (9)
Barclay Junior School

The Street

When the night comes the street lights look over us like a mother looking down on her baby,
The cars zoom down the road with the speed of a thousand cheetahs,
The rubbish in the dustbin whispers 'Let me out, let me out' like people stuck in a lift,
Then when the children leave their homes to go to school their footsteps on the pavement tap, like tap dancers tap dancing
The people out at late-night parties roar like hungry lions waiting to eat their prey.
The gates outside bang like someone playing a tambourine 'Bang, Bang'
The tree's leaves rustle like paper being crunched into a ball
The wind howls like a wolf mourning for its dead in the middle of the night
The car horns toot like a wise owl perched on the branch of a tree.

All these actions and things take place
Right in front of our faces
Yet we pass and do not realise
They are connected to other parts of our lives.

Adiah Mellad (10)
Barclay Junior School

Keep On Dancing People

Do the tango baby, do it now 'cause if you don't you won't know how.

Do the jazz people, do it the same, 'cause if you don't you'll be lame.

So keep on dancing ladies and gentlemen.
But if you get bored come another dancing day.

Azam Rashid (9)
Barclay Junior School

What If?

What if the world turned square?
Would you care?
No, you wouldn't.

What if cats roared?
Would you be bored?
No, you wouldn't.

What if trees grew money?
Would that be funny?
Yes, it would.

What if aliens wore spotted crowns?
Would that be allowed?
No, it wouldn't.

What if you were rich
Or owned a football pitch?
Would that matter?
No I guess it wouldn't.

What if everything stayed the same?
Would that be a good game?
No, that would be boring.
I'd be snoring.
But that's the way the world's going to stay.

Naomi Black (9)
Barclay Junior School

Blue

Blue is a colour of the rainbow
And the colour of the sky
Blue is the colour of joy and peace.

Rehana Udat (9)
Barclay Junior School

There Was A Young Man

There was a young man who went to Spain
But he didn't know what to say
So they took him to jail tied him with chains
Then he looked in the sky
And he got shy
Next he cried
And he sighed.

Lucky Acan (9)
Barclay Junior School

My Country

I left my country but . . .
I'll never forget it
I cry every day and
I don't win anything.
Somebody says your country is bad,
But,
I never believe them
Because my country is the best for me.

Enea Ali (10)
Barclay Junior School

The Dinner Plate

As everyone is lining up for dinner
Should we have spaghetti in tomato sauce?
Just like worms in mud or peas that are so mushy and yucky
Or cookies that look like round apples with maggots coming out from inside?
But I just decided to have sausages, beans and chips.

Kali Greaves (10)
Barclay Junior School

THE ADVENTURE PLAYGROUND

The playground was big as the universe
The children were running like a herd of cheetahs
The climbing frame was colourful as a peacock's feathers
The bricks were old as an old man,
The sky was blue as bluebells,
The trees were wavy as sea,
The whistle was loud as a trumpet,
The children turned up, growling like lions.

Gloria Musoke (8)
Barclay Junior School

HOMEWORK

H is for homework, for good or for bad,
O is for obedience, so says my dad,
M is for maths, the thing I hate most,
E is for English, I'll finish after my toast
W is for writing, I can never get mine straight,
O is for occasionally bringing it in late,
R is for reading, Harry Potter and other stuff
K is for kindness, when Dad finishes mine off.

Bethany West (8)
Barclay Junior School

THE HOLLOW MAN

If you dare to approach his dark lair
The hollow man will chop off your hair
He crushes your bones and puts them in the basement
He's waiting . . . just waiting . . . to get you.

He has an evil smile on his face
He'll hit you hard with his mace
He's always going to be there waiting
He's waiting . . . just waiting . . . to get you.

Sannah Ahmed & Mahum (9)
Barclay Junior School

THE VAMPIRE

He lives in a slimy, horrible, bloody cave
You would not dare to step in his cave
He's braver, so brave, braver than you
He's waiting . . . just waiting . . . to get you!
He has horrible, sharp fangs
And big hairy hands and drinks pints of blood
He's waiting . . . just waiting . . .. to get you!

Yasmin Shah (9)
Barclay Junior School

THE STRANGE SEA

The sea is deep
The sea is like a hungry dot
If someone goes in a ship it will take so long.
There's gold under the sea
The sea is lonely and enormous
It's more deep than before.
Lots of sea creatures have died under water
And their eyes have turned into pearls
And lots of secrets lie under the sea.

Humza Adnan Darr (9)
Barclay Junior School

PLAYTIME

P laytime is cool,
L aughter, chattering in the playground,
A fter play time it's no more fun,
Y elling, shouting when it's time to play.

T ime to go in (ohhhhh)
I love the playground
M e and my friends playing
E veryone happy.

Amy Spink (9)
Barclay Junior School

FISH

There was once a girl called Lish
Who wanted a wish
So that she could have a fish
That played on a dish
She was in the water flishing
She was in the sea twishing.

Saima Ali (10)
Barclay Junior School

WINTER

W hite is the colour of falling snow
I cicles are forming on the ground below
N othing is left on the old oak tree
T ime for the animals to hibernate
E verybody in their houses, wrapped up nice and warm
R eading Christmas stories of when Jesus was born.

Kate Brooks (9)
Barclay Junior School

Drifting Through Space

There's Neptune that was discovered in 1846
While I go past I see birth of a new born star,
There I see Neil Armstrong put first foot on the moon.

There goes the Milky Way nice and colourful
I can hear the stars explode,
I can see a comet going through the sky.

The sun is so bright I can't bare to look at it,
And there's Mars as orange as Jupiter,
Now I am going back to Earth.

Aysha Patel (11)
Barclay Junior School

The Moon

The moon stands high in the sky
It only comes at night
The first man to land on the moon
Was Neil Armstrong in 1969.
There is about over eighteen moons
It doesn't come out at noon,
The full moon is the bright
It hasn't got a lot of weight,
The moon is shiny like silver,
But it will never sliver,
Because it is the second nearest to the sun.
It is not made of cheese in a bun,
But it's probably got cheese.

Mustafa Ersalan (11)
Barclay Junior School

The Hairy Vampire

In a horrible, nasty, dark, fearsome cave . . .
Watch out for the silvery hairy vampire called Dave
It's the vampire that you will never want to trust
But it's waiting . . . but why waiting?
To bite you.

He will turn into a bat
That you've never seen
That's hairy and fat
You will see the slivering blood dripping down
It's waiting why?
You know now just waiting . . . to get you.

Usman Akram & Emre Korkmaz (9)
Barclay Junior School

My Uncle And I

My uncle and I
Have a great time together
Just like when I beat him at bowling
But not snooker or pool
When he talks I laugh for some reason.

My uncle and I
Go mad sometimes
But never as mad as my mum
But as mad as a computer indeed,
But no one knows why.

Karim Pritchard (9)
Barclay Junior School

The Wild Sea

The sea is so nice and smooth
Sometimes the sea can make big waves with its strong waters.
Sometimes children fight with their water boards
Only the fish can stay under the water for long
Children tell each other jokes at the seaside
Children say water is grey, the grown-ups say the water is blue
The sea has a special secret that nobody knows.
Ships that have sunken have changed into coral
The sea holds many mysteries and stories that are untold.

Adnan Mahmood (8)
Barclay Junior School

Happiness

Happiness is the colour light pink
It smells like someone who's just had a bath,
It sounds like pop music,
It tastes like sweets and everything sugary,
It looks like children playing,
It feels like soft fur,
And it lives in your heart.

Uzmah Rashid (9)
Barclay Junior School

Computer

So many computer games
I can't get through the lot
I've been trying for days and days
And now my computer's hot.

Amaan Javed (10)
Barclay Junior School

School Daze

Our school day starts with playground chaos
With children racing and people talking
Now there's the teacher who strides on time
She opens her lips to request us to rise and shine
But outside a boy is late, he won't get here at this rate
Much later on the teacher is mad when I stopped talking she was glad.

The doors slam the teacher shouts
As pencils and books get thrown about
The zoos must have a calmer way
But every day is a real school daze.

Sujawal Sharif (11)
Barclay Junior School

Riddles

I am as stunning as anything
And as precious as a rose.
I'm as bright as the sunset
And I come a few times in this season.
I am the last of many,
But there are more to come.
When the sun comes out,
While the rain falls
That's when my work is done.

Rainbow.

Uzma Nasir (10)
Barclay Junior School

A Day In The Life Of A Lazy Man

Sits on the couch,
Plays a video game,
Goes to the pub,
Has a large meal,
Eats a quarter pounder,
Sits on the couch,
Plays a video,
Finds a cosy chair,
Has a nice nap,
Eats a quarter pounder.

Richard Burrowes (9)
Barclay Junior School

Riddle

I'm in you,
You see me every day,
I fall out when I want,
But without me you'll have a big stomach ache,
When you get old you take me out like stars at night.

Waqar Riaz (11)
Barclay Junior School

The Dirty Man

There was a man who lived in a bin
He had a mum made out of tin
The man ate garbage for his lunch
And ate it with a big, fat crunch.

Michele Clarke (9)
Barclay Junior School

Best Friends

Best friends are forever
We stick together
Even when life is rough
We stand together tough.

We have sleepovers
We go rollerblading, skating
We do gymnastics, it's fantastic.

We have fun together,
We laugh at each other's jokes,
I hope this goes on forever and ever!

Katie Stone (9) & Zakiyah Rawat (8)
Barclay Junior School

A Day In The Life Of Stone Cold

Stone Cold fights,
Has a rest,
Drinks his beer,
Goes to his room
And sleeps.

Stone Cold fights,
Has a rest,
Talks to The Rock,
Practices fighting
And sleeps.

Junaid Elahi (9) & Saad Nasir (8)
Barclay Junior School

Cats And Birds

Cats
Curled claws
And ears listening carefully
Taking toys
Silver eyes like stars.

Birds
They fly in the sky
They twit-ta-whoo in the night
And some feed on seeds.

Dayo Mwangi (8)
Barclay Junior School

The Sun

It tastes as hot as chilli sauce,
It looks like a smily face,
It sounds like crying,
It feels like fire,
It smells like smoke.

Anees Imtiaz (9)
Barclay Junior School

Sun And Play

It was a fine sunny day
In the month of May
It was a fine time for everyone to come out and play
Everyone was thankful that it was a nice day.

Faisal Pervaze (10)
Barclay Junior School

Love Of Life

Your name is so sweet you make my heart beat
Thinking of you night and day
That this feeling will never fade away
Love and tender are together
Commitment to your love
Bless from above
Your love is so strong like fire burning
The hotness inside you is turning
Your heart's sweet like a feather
Explore yourself with love and tender.

Parul Motin (10)
Barclay Junior School

My Sister

My sister is a blister whenever I need to go to the loo
I see her doing a poo!
Whenever I go downstairs I see her wearing flares!
When I go upstairs then I have to wear flares!
That's my sister
Who's a very big blister.

Yasir Hussain (9)
Barclay Junior School

The Golden Sea

The sea is calm on a bright golden day
And children and parents come and make a sand castle
And splash in the water
On a rich, silvery, bright day.

Nazia Ali (9)
Barclay Junior School

Storm

I made a twister that snatched a house off the ground
I pushed an aeroplane into my twister
I pushed an air balloon into the ocean with no escape
I made another twister into the ocean
So that the sea creatures and the air balloon died
I burned a whole tree down with just one lightning shock
I lifted over one million buildings in the air
I started to die down weaker and weaker by the minute
Then I just vanished into thin air.

Jamiah Ahkeen Baker (9)
Barclay Junior School

Spring

S ome of the world is getting warm
P eople and animals are being born
R oosters are making noise across the farms
I n houses people are feeling more bright and happy
N ice flowers are beginning to grow
G ardeners all around are planting flowers for summer.

Natalie Small (9) & Roxanne Lawrence (8)
Barclay Junior School

Rain

Rain is water, soggy and wet,
Rain comes anytime when it's set
Rain falls on animals like a pet,
Rain makes you ill,
So you have to go to Dudleyville.

Jazib Syed (9)
Barclay Junior School

TEACHERS

In the dark, horrible staffroom where the teachers stare
If you dare to go in there
Many have gone in there but not one has come out alive
They're waiting . . . just waiting . . . to give you a detention!

Teachers with the big heads and curly hair
They will never be fair
Their brainy heads and their wretched skin
Oh they're waiting . . . oh yes . . . just waiting . . .
To give you a detention.

Michael Delew (8) & Zan Saleem (9)
Barclay Junior School

MY PETS

My pet cat likes to claw the mat,
My pet fish likes to swim in a dish,
My pet rabbit has a really bad habit,
My pet dog likes to jump on a log,
My pet hamster is brown and white
And stays awake all through the night.

Jade Eve (9)
Barclay Junior School

THE NONSENSE LADY

There was a young lady called Nelly
Who liked to eat red jelly
One day she went to Devon
And the next day she came down from Heaven
And that was the end of Nelly with her big fat jelly belly.

Melissa Bolessa (10)
Barclay Junior School

Wind

Have you heard the wind blowing through the air?
Sometimes the wind it whistles through the air
Sometimes the wind is very windy
It blows me away in the night
The wind blows me away
The wind blows very loud
And it scares me when I'm in bed
It rains with the wind.

Dexter Christie (9)
Barclay Junior School

It's Playtime!

The buzzer sounds like a buzzy bee
And that's when we know it's playtime
The children run as fast as cheetahs
The climbing frame is as colourful as the rainbow
The ground is as hard as metal
We are stuck in the playground, we feel like prisoners.

Shahid Mangera (8)
Barclay Junior School

Calm Blue

Calm is the colour blue,
Blue is as calm as the warm sky above us,
Blue is the colour of the blue, gentle, salty sea,
Blue is as pretty as the bluebell in a wonderful forest,
Blue is as calm as the angels that float around us,
Blue is as soft as calm.

Sarah Sappong (9)
Barclay Junior School

I May Be . . .

I may be young,
I may be old,
I may be strong,
I may be weak,
I may be good,
I may be bad,
I may be short,
I may be tall,
I may be big,
I may be little,
But deep inside I'm still a child.

Samiya Najib (9)
Barclay Junior School

The Land Of The Sandament Sum

In the land of Sandament Sum
The people all joke and hum
They never vote for mayor
Or ever cut their hair
What a place for someone dumb
In the land of Sandament Sum
You can buy hot rocks from the sun
They give away packets of stew
From a large animal zoo
That's the land of Sandament Sum.

Nnamdi Odiaka (10)
Barclay Junior School

Swimming In The Sea

S wimming in the sea
E ating lots of ice cream
A nts crawling up and down
S andcastles we are making
I ce is what I need
D rinking all the cola
E nding our visit we say goodbye.

Safia Kayani (8)
Barclay Junior School

The Ship

The creek of oars
The squeak of mice,
The sea shanty of drunken men
The faint barking of seals
The cannon's roar when we go into war
And we come home from war
Ready for a good load of food and a good night's sleep!

Bryony Kay (9)
Barclay Junior School

Animals

A nimals are the best
N ow animals are cool
I like pandas
M aggots are disgusting
A panda eats bamboo
L ions are nice.

Alistair Burlinson (7)
Barclay Junior School

I Love Red

Red is as red as a heart,
It's as sparkling as glass,
It's as red as a rose,
It's as warm as blood,
It's as nice as a flower,
It's as red as a red felt tip pen,
It's lovely and relaxing,
It's love,
When you really love someone.

Aisha Ahmad (9)
Barclay Junior School

Fireworks

F ireworks sparkling in the night
I t's bonfire night
R ed and green fireworks
E veryone's having fun
W hizzing around are fireworks
O pen the packets of fireworks
R ockets flying in the dark sky
K eep safe and don't run
S tars all over the sky.

Maryam Choudhry (8)
Barclay Junior School

HURRICANE

H owling through the trees
U mbrellas get blown away
R ain tumbling down
R ushing through the valleys
I nside their homes people will hide
C ats and dogs get terrified
A nd run inside
N ow trees crash down
E ventually it stops and the town is left a wreck.

Emma Scully (9)
Barclay Junior School

THE DREAM OF A WONDER WORLD

The clear, turquoise sea,
of what I wish of,
Its everlasting words,
with its ripples up above.
The gold coin reflects at the moon,
with great rays of honour,
looking down at the sea.
I could hear laughing,
and see happiness.
With the touch of splashes,
of sapphire dreamlight.
Mother Nature doing her duty,
while fireflies,
happily giving her light.
Clouds that are soft and delicate,
with fluff that are,
fantasy with mystique.

Sneh Brahmbhatt (9)
Berger Primary School

WHAT'S THE TIME MISS?

What's the time Miss? I can't see what's the time Miss
Is it twenty past three?
I'm in class again still not having fun,
Maybe I will have a dream of me in the sun.
Aren't you hungry Jenny? It's time to go
I hate school dinners oh no.
What's the time Miss? I can't see what's the time Miss?
Is it twenty past three.
It's time to eat the food that makes me feel ill.
It's time for the afters, that will change how I feel.
What's the time Miss? I can't see, what's the time Miss?
Is it twenty past three?

Jennifer Starling (9)
Berger Primary School

DAY AND NIGHT

Sunny day,
Sunny day how I love a sunny day.
I like the sun,
I like the breeze,
I like birds singing in the trees.

Dark night,
Dark night,
How I love a dark night.
I like the moon,
I like the stars,
I like eating chocolate bars.

Daniel Ekelegbu (11)
Berger Primary School

I WISH

How I wish I were tall,
and the world around me
small.
With my head in the sky,
I'd see aeroplanes go by.
I'd have a special chair in
class,
and in all my tests I'd
always pass.

Temitope Olowu (8)
Berger Primary School

A CLOWN

A clown went to the town, to see Queen's crown.
But his pants fell down, and made him blush brown.
The Queen lost her crown.

Alastair Cary (9)
Berger Primary School

MY ONE AND ONLY MUM

I love you, I love you,
I hope you love me too.
You're the only one who's special
You're the only one I choose.

No one knows how much I love you
My love for you is true.
Every time I look at you
I know that you will always do.

Aysha Begum (10)
Canon Barnett Primary School

The Key To My Heart

The key, the key
To my heart
The key, the key,
You are the one.
The key, the key,
You let me gaze
Speechlessly at my mum.

Key, oh key
Please give me the key,
To my heart,
Which has my beautiful
Mother in it.
Oh please, oh please,
Give me the key,
I love my mum forever and ever.

Oh Mum, Oh Mum,
My wonderful mum,
The key is in your heart,
And it is always going to stay like that.

Sayeeda Qureshi (11)
Canon Barnett Primary School

The One And Only Love Of My Life!

(For My Dad)

I love you,
Only you.
You're the best
No one but you.

Missing you,
Day and night,
Never being able to see you.

Dreaming of you,
Everywhere I go.
You're the one and only,
Love of my life!

Sabah Mahmood (10)
Canon Barnett Primary School

HAUNTED BY SORROW!

The touch of the tears,
Brings out cries,
Protecting the fears,
Beneath the earth, it lies.

As the times fade away,
Memories at the corner of your heart,
It hasn't been discovered for a time in a day,
It's never to be apart.

Darkness deep under the soul,
Happens to be terrified,
Missing the precious hole,
Nowhere and no reason to hide.

Why they pass away, must be for a reason,
Sometimes it matters how you feel,
Releasing it through the seasons,
Sometimes you want to kneel.

Tearing your heart into a flame,
Sinking in your mind about the past,
Never forgetting that you got the blame,
From the last moment of your life.
The very last!

Farhana Rahman (10)
Canon Barnett Primary School

Loneliness

Loneliness is to be alone.
Nobody to talk to.
Nobody to have as a friend,
Nobody to make you laugh.
No one can make you smile.
No one but a true friend.
I never knew how it felt
To have a best friend.
I see a boy approaching me,
But he might just pass me by.
He didn't stop and put me ahead
Of my loneliness.
But still left me behind.

Saadi Salam (10)
Canon Barnett Primary School

Fear

It was a dark and evil night,
For your soul and your heart.
As you shiver full of fear,
Your mind is being taken over.

When you tremble full of fright,
The evil around you comes out and haunts.
As you think of what you did
You stop feeling the pleasure of fear.

Now that your mind has been taken over,
There is no place to hide and run.
It will haunt you,
Until the day you are destroyed!
Beware, fear can kill.

Rehan Rafiq (11)
Canon Barnett Primary School

The Love Of My Life

The love of my life
That I have known so long.

I have seen her
Since I was born.

She has been with me
As long as I lived.

I have seen her
I have been with her.

She has always been there for me
And never against me.

She is the only
Love of my life.

Shahana Begum (11)
Canon Barnett Primary School

In The Park

Dogs barking,
Cars parking,
Children talking,
People walking,
Babies crying,
Children lying,
People funny,
Eating honey.
People racing,
Cars pacing.
Kids lazy,
Mothers crazy.

Rebeka Khanum (9)
Old Palace Primary School

The Dragon

The dragon is as big as a mountain,
It is brave, fierce and scary.
The dragon has long, sharp teeth and claws,
The teeth and claws are as white as snow.
The dragon has a big, hot flame on its tail,
The dragon breathes fire,
It is as hot as lava.

The dragon's scales are green as grass,
They shine like silver.
The dragon's scales glisten like the moon
And stars in the dark night sky.

As the dragon walks it makes a sound,
Thud,
Thud,
Thud.

Dildar Hussain (11)
Old Palace Primary School

Babies

Babies! Babies! Babies!
What are they?
My little sister
Cries every day.

Flying dinners,
Nappies too.
All the headaches
You don't know what to do.

Rocking crib
Toys on the floor
Makes you wonder
If there's anymore!

Rajna Miah (11)
Old Palace Primary School

My Mother

I love my mother.
She is always there when I need her.
When I trip over and cut my knee, she comforts me.
When I'm in a fight, she takes my side.
When I have a problem, she answers it.

I love my mother.
She is always there when I need her.
When it is my birthday, she buys me presents.
When I'm lonely, she gives me company.
When I cry, she wipes my tears.

I love my mother.
She is always there when I need her.
When I sneeze, she hands me a tissue.
When I forget my lunch, she brings it to me.
When I get stuck on my homework, she helps me.

I love my mother.
She is always there when I need her.

Lubna Rahman (11)
Old Palace Primary School

I LIKE . . .

I like the way worms wriggle,
The light blue sky,
I like the green grass,
Everyone asks me why.

I think spiders are okay,
And my friends are really cool,
I like to play outside a lot,
And jump in the swimming pool.

I like the way children laugh,
And play all day,
They always have fun with me,
Maybe they want to play today.

Some people think I'm crazy,
And very very weird,
Maybe I'm like this,
Because I've got a purple beard.

Roxanne Kumalo (10)
Old Palace Primary School

FOOTBALL

Miss Molloy scoring
Miss Morris screaming
Fans singing
People cheering
Referee shouting
Defenders blocking
Babies crying
Hearts beating and
Man U Winning!

Shubona B Ali (8)
Old Palace Primary School

Super Blast

I'm gliding, gliding up and up into the sky,
Blasting off at the speed of light.
Surrender now or prepare to fight.
As the speed slackens to an end,
I feel as if I'm going round the bend.
I see the marvellous sight of planet Zorg.
It looks nauseous but I remain cautious.
Remember no rocket is better than . . .
    Super Blast.

Alethea Raban (8)
Old Palace Primary School

Egyptians

Pulling the brain out through the nose
Is the way it goes.

Washing the body with wine or vinegar
Is bad enough, but leaving it for forty days is daft.

Stuffing the body with linen
The person must be a villain.

Will the body really crack?
Just in case we'll oil and spice it
Before we wrap the face.

If you spend fifteen days wrapping the body
In bandages, you'll have a mummy.

Put in a painted box now
The mummy is ready,
All you have to say is ready steady go.

Hannah Chowdhury (9)
Shaftesbury Primary School

Apocalypse!

Help! Help! The Apocalypse is here,
Our houses are on fire
We can smell the fiery air.

Pray! Pray! You go to Heaven
Not to Hell,
The Devil will seek you.

We need more time to run.
There they are the Skele men,
Throwing balls of fire, chasing everyone.

Run! Run! Run! for your lives.
They will come for you and haunt you.

Help! Help! There you are,
It's finally the end, goodbye.
I say goodbye.

Sharan Matharu (10)
Shaftesbury Primary School

Season Haikus

Spring Haiku
Blossom trees are here
And new flowers are growing
Birds are coming back.

Summer Haiku
Summer is here now
Butterflies are in the sky
It is boiling hot.

Autumn Haiku
Autumn is here now
Leaves are falling on the ground
Gold, red and green leaves.

Winter Haiku
Winter is so cold
Children are building snowmen
Snowflakes are falling.

Saira Khan (9)
Shaftesbury Primary School

MIXED SOUNDS

The hissing of a snake,
The slurping of a cake,
The clang of the dishes,
The splash of the fishes.

The stomp of a dragon,
The rattling of a wagon,
The swoosh of a storm,
The ripping of a form.

The sprinkle of the glitter
And the shuffling of the litter.

We hope you remember
And treasure these things
And one more thing,
The jingling of the rings.

Diana Kurakina (11)
Shaftesbury Primary School

TEACHERS

Have you ever seen your teacher smoking?
Smoking behind your back.
Making sure that you're not knowing,
Making sure that they don't get the sack.

Have you ever seen your teacher in a pub?
In a pub drinking beer?
I thought teachers go to a youth club,
But in school they call you a dear.

Have you ever seen your teacher acting cool?
Acting cool in the street?
In my spare time I normally go to the pool,
I've banged my head and found it was made of concrete.

Rabi Niam (10)
Shaftesbury Primary School

AUTUMN'S THE BEST

Autumn's the best yes I'm right,
I like autumn plus my favourite colour white.
Autumn's the best I must request,
Autumn's cold so I wear very thick vests.
Autumn's the best I definitely think,
When the wind blows hard I have to blink.
Autumn's the best I have to say
I love the way the trees sway.
Autumn's the best that's my request
Why should I worry because autumn's the best.

Christopher Palmer (10)
Shaftesbury Primary School

I Wonder Why?

I wonder why the grass is green,
And the wind is never seen?

Who taught the birds to make a nest,
And taught the trees to take a rest?

Who made the sky,
And who taught us to buy?

How did earthquakes come,
And how did things become?

Why is the blood red,
And why are there beds?

How is the world made,
Why are people so mad?

How are languages being made,
And how are they said?

Rohini Solanki (9)
Shaftesbury Primary School

Fire

Fire! Fire! Burning bright.
Fire! Fire! Ready to fight.
Fire! Fire! Count to four.
Fire! Fire! Nothing more.

Fire! Fire! Colours are bright.
Fire! Fire! Burning on the night.
Fire! Fire! Really freaky.
Fire! Fire! Getting creepy.

Eunice Maina (9)
Shaftesbury Primary School

Jealousy

Jealousy is black and blue
It smells like a smelly shoe
Tastes like yucky glue
Sounds like someone doing poo
Feels like I want to punch you
And where it lives, well deep inside you.

Arpit Vyas (10)
Shaftesbury Primary School

Happiness

Happiness is light pink
Happiness smells like chocolate
Happiness tastes like fresh water
Happiness sounds like children laughing
Happiness feels like air
Happiness lives in Heaven.

Radhea Rahman (10)
Shaftesbury Primary School

Fractions

Fractions are the best
Fractions make your brains clever.
They make you clever as a bee.

Maths makes you good at work
Maths is easy.
Maths is like people fighting over things.

Gulam Hussain (9)
Shaftesbury Primary School

WINTER

The wind is blowing
My hands are going numb
Red noses are everywhere
Your nose is always runny
Snowflakes are falling everywhere
On top of all of you.

Nishma Parekh (10)
Shaftesbury Primary School

FRIENDSHIP

It is like glittering gold
It smells like fresh flowers
It tastes like a box of chocolates
It sounds like loud music
It feels like cuddly teddy bears
It lives in the summer.

Neelam Kaur (10)
Shaftesbury Primary School

FRIENDSHIP

Friendship is the colour of gold.
Friendship smells like a bar of chocolate.
Friendship tastes like pizza.
Friendship sounds like someone singing with you.
Friendship feels like you're on top of the world.
Friendship lives in your heart.

Sherita Bukkar (9)
Shaftesbury Primary School

Winter Poem

Winter has come with snow
It is trying to help us get a cold
Never let snow on your face
Tell us not to play in snowball fights.
Everybody has red cheeks
Running around playing with snow.

Akkash Purani (10)
Shaftesbury Primary School

Hope

Hope is a rainbow
It smells like a flower
It tastes like chocolate
It sounds like music
It feels soft and fluffy
It lives in the clouds.

Almas Zaman (9)
Shaftesbury Primary School

Friendship

Friendship is like gold
Friendship smells like chocolate cake
Friendship tastes like sweets
Friendship sounds like birds singing
Friendship feels like paradise
Friendship lives in your heart.

Anisha Mansuri (10)
Shaftesbury Primary School

HAPPINESS

Happiness is light blue
And smells like roses.
Happiness tastes like it is made of sugar
And sounds like a sparrow's chirp.
Happiness feels like velvet running through your fingers
And lives at the bottom of your heart.

Jon Pell (10)
Shaftesbury Primary School

HAPPINESS

Happiness is the colour of yellow
It smells like grown flowers
It tastes like chicken
It sounds like birds singing
It feels like you are flying on clouds.
It lives in the sun.

Shane Anthony (9)
Shaftesbury Primary School

HAPPINESS

Happiness is the colour of yellow
It smells like a flower
It tastes like Sunny Delight
It sounds like someone is laughing
It feels like you are flying
It lives in a house.

Muhammed Haq (10)
Shaftesbury Primary School

Thinking About Autumn

Leaves go brown
Leaves fall off trees.
Lots of leaves on the floor
I can hear them whispering 'I am free.'

In autumn it's fun
Kick about
Golden and brown leaves
To run and shout.

Krupa Patel (10)
Shaftesbury Primary School

Life Is Worthless For Me

For me life is worthless for me.
I have no family to turn to.
Now I am an orphan.

I work in a workhouse day and night
With little food.
I only wanted more, but I ended up with this.

This being weak, feeling lonely
Sleeping with dead people.
How I wish I was in that coffin.

Life is worthless for me
For other boys are loved by their family.
I wish I could rest in peace,
And my life would not be so dark and gloomy.

Who am I? I don't know who I am anymore.
As I have been saying, life is worthless for me.

Damola Taiwo (8)
St Luke's Primary School

FEELINGS

Happiness is yellow,
It feels like fun,
And it tastes like pizza.
Happiness smells like pollen,
It sounds like cheery children,
And it looks like a butterfly flittering to and fro.

Love is wine-coloured
It feels like milk,
And it tastes like Galaxy chocolate.
Love smells like roses,
It sounds like birds whistling,
And it looks like a beautiful face.

Fear is black,
It feels like a jagged rock,
And it tastes like worms.
Fear smells like manure,
It sounds like an echoing haunted voice,
And it looks like a ghoul.

Madness is multi-coloured,
It feels like twirls in your head,
And it tastes like popping candy.
Madness smells like coffee
It sounds like ninety nine million people
Talking to you at once,
And it looks like a washing machine
Going round and round.

Trudy Mensah (9)
St Luke's Primary School

FEELINGS

Happiness
Happiness is yellow,
It sounds like birds chirping merrily,
It looks like flowers growing in a garden,
It tastes like strawberries and cream,
It feels like an exciting adventure.

Love
Love is red,
It sounds like dolphins swimming in the sea.
It looks like roses,
It tastes like sweet apple pie.
It feels romantic.

Madness
Madness is multi-coloured,
It sounds like people laughing and never stopping,
It looks like someone spinning around forever,
It tastes like ice cream,
It feels like you're going crazy.

Chelsie Spagnol (8)
St Luke's Primary School

MY MONSTER

My monster is as funny as a clown
He is as messy as a baby
He is as annoying as an itchy sweater
His hair is as spiky as spikes.
His arms are as thin as twigs.
His ears are as sharp as sharp knives.
He has a mouth as big as five tennis balls.
He has eyebrows as bushy as bushes.

James Marstin (9)
St Luke's Primary School

My Weird Mummy

My weird Mum's eyes
are as big as a ball.

My weird Mum's teeth
are as big as a king's.

My weird Mum's hand
is as big as a gun.

My weird Mum's knees
are as big as a tennis ball.

My weird Mum's legs
are as big as an elephant.

My weird Mum's feet
are as big as a river.

My weird Mum's hair
is as big as a gorilla.

My weird Mum's glasses
are as wet as a river.

Elyse Daniells (8)
St Luke's Primary School

The Beach

The sea waved as the sun shone.
The sand crumbled as the children played.
As the rain fell and the water rose,
The wind blew and the beach ball rolled.
The seashells were collected.

Jacey Johnson (9)
St Luke's Primary School

The Snowman

My first sign of life is when I can see,
I spy a small boy, who is dancing with glee.
He places a carrot on my face for a nose,
Then gives me three buttons to give an impression of clothes.

The wind it is howling, the snow's falling fast,
I stand tall and proud like a sailing boat's mast.
The little boy's fingers and cheeks turn bright red,
But before going in he puts a hat on my head.

The very next morning I awake with a fright,
The temperature changed at the end of the night.
The sun's rays beating down on my back, it is felt
And slowly but surely I am starting to melt.

Simon Bradshaw (8)
St Luke's Primary School

Happiness

Happiness feels like children playing around in the park.
Happiness sounds like birds singing around you.
Happiness tastes like sweet chocolates melting in your mouth.
Happiness looks like a newborn baby.
Happiness feels like a new soft teddy.
Happiness sounds like raindrops dropping on the floor.
Happiness tastes like sweet cherries.
Happiness looks like a beautiful puppy.
Happiness feels like a snowflake melting on your nose.
Happiness is the best thing anyone could ever have.

Nicola Rodrigues (9)
St Luke's Primary School

Billy The Vampire

Billy the vampire has claws as sharp as knives.
He's got one ear as small as a goldfish.
His other ear is as big as a killer piranha.
His legs are as thin as pens.
He is as fierce as three tigers and three lions.
His nose is as big as a tennis ball.
His voice is as loud as fifty two trumpets
Playing at the same time.

Joe Robinson (9)
St Luke's Primary School

The Beggar's Song!

Neither house nor bed have I
But I beg on my box
And I have
Dogs, dogs, dogs!

Neither friends nor family have I
But I sleep on the floor
And I have
Dogs, dogs, dogs!

Neither notes nor coins have I
But I eat on my box
And I have
Dogs, dogs, dogs.

Neither shoes nor clothes have I
But I have two tiny dogs,
And I have
Companions!

Eleanor Bramley (9)
St Mary's RC Primary School

RABBIT BOY!

For days and days the boy he smiled,
Smiling at all he saw.
I'm not a boy at all he said,
As he ran through the door.

One day his dad went on the lawn,
And to his great surprise,
His son was eating all the grass,
In front of his very eyes.

'I'm not a boy anymore,' he said.
'Eating grass is my habit.
I do not have to go to school,
Because now I am a rabbit.'

Eleanor Bramley (9)
St Mary's RC Primary School

LOVE FROM A DOVE

Neither scales nor fins have I,
But I glide with my songs.
And I have,
Beauty, beauty, beauty!

Neither prickles nor hate have I,
But I flow softly with the wind.
And I have,
Beauty, beauty, beauty!

Neither horn nor hoofs have I,
But I have many talents,
And I have
Beauty, beauty, beauty!

Genevieve Karacochi (9)
St Mary's RC Primary School

The Balloon Song

Neither sight nor hearing have I
But I fly on my string
And I have
Helium, Helium, Helium!

Thomas Gissane (9)
St Mary's RC Primary School

What A Load Of Nonsense

'Twas dingy and the stinky rats
Did squeak and demolish in the swamp;
All suspicious were the sunflowers
And the indestructible crocs sneezed.

Victoria Maddock (9)
St Mary's RC Primary School

The Shark Song

Neither fingers nor feet have I
But I swim through seas
And I have
Hunger, hunger, hunger.

Clare Brennan (9)
St Mary's RC Primary School

The Spaceman Song

Neither fur nor horns have I
But I jump on the moon
And I have
A suit, a suit, a suit!

Mary-Anne Murray (10)
St Mary's RC Primary School

The Mongoose Song

Neither horns nor fins have I
But I sprint on my paws
And I have
Teeth, teeth, teeth!

Luke Walters (10)
St Mary's RC Primary School

The Monkey Song

Neither fur nor tongue have I
But I swing on my paws
And I have
Talent, talent, talent.

David Gannaway (9)
St Mary's RC Primary School

The Tiger Song

Neither leaves nor fingers have I
But I attack on my feet,
And I have,
Claws, claws, claws.

Neither horns nor roots have I
But I kill with my teeth,
And I have
Claws, claws, claws.

Neither wings nor fins have I
But I run with my feet
And I have
Claws, claws, claws.

Christopher Hodges (10)
St Mary's RC Primary School

Teachers

Teachers working
They are working very hard
One was eating a gherkin
And walking with a plain card.

Teachers in the staffroom
All rushing about
Coming so soon
And turning to the route.

Teachers all walking
Very hard to think
All chatters and talking
And starting to blink.

Jacqueline Marie (9)
St Mary's RC Primary School

THE PUPPY SONG

Neither wings nor fins have I
But I run on my four legs
And I have
Fur, fur, fur!

Neither guns nor speech have I,
But I run like the wind
And I have
Fur, fur, fur!

Neither horns nor hooves have I
But I can jump high
And I have
Fur, fur, fur!

Michael Young (10)
St Mary's RC Primary School

PETS

Dogs here, dogs there,
Dogs, dogs, everywhere.
Dogs are cute (unlike a newt),
Dogs are playful but sometimes painful.

Cats here, cats there
Cats, cats, everywhere
Cats are quick and have a nice lick
Cats are cool but certainly don't rule.

Hamsters here, hamsters there,
Hamsters, hamsters, everywhere.
Hamsters are small and like to be in a ball
Hamsters are fast and will rush past.

Alex Mulhern (9)
St Mary's RC Primary School

SCHOOL

St Mary's School is OK
Learning things day by day.

Teachers are good
They teach us well.

Dinner ladies feed us
They make us swell.

Kids are funny
They change each day.

Nasty nasty lots to say
Bullies, bullies stay away.

Why be nasty day by day?
Ain't got nothing nice to say.

So you bullies stay well away.

Claire Hannon (9)
St Mary's RC Primary School

SUMMER POEM

In the summer it is hot
In the summer you go on holiday
In the summer you go to the beach
In the summer you can play
In the summer you can play sports
In the summer you go swimming
In the summer you can celebrate
In the summer you go to the park
In the summer you can play cricket
In the summer you can sunbathe.

Keith Brown (8)
St Mary's RC Primary School

ANIMALS!

Animals have that kind of personality
Like when you wash your car and it goes white.
And your garden looks like it's been blown up by dynamite
But worst of all you still have to look after your
Pets!

Pets just make a mess
Like when you give it a bath and then you go to the forest
And when it chews up your brand new dress,
They act like they're
Wild!

Wild animals just don't care
Like when they stamp over your favourite flower
And they walk over the wet paint that took you over an hour
I just can't cope with all these
Animals!

Kate Parker (9)
St Mary's RC Primary School

MY SCHOOL IS GREAT

My school is wonderful
It is great
I love it so much
And I'm never late.
Anne's handwriting's so neat
Our school is so good,
And sometimes we eat meat.
Miss Pluncket has a ponytail
And she wears it up all day.
We try to understand her in a way.

Hollie Wells (7)
St Mary's RC Primary School

THE MONTHS OF THE YEAR

January brings the snow
makes the children grow.

February brings the rain
and makes us grow again.

March brings the breeze
and it makes us sneeze.

April sees a lot of showers
and shows its powers.

May today you have to pay
tomorrow you have to pray.

June is my dad's year
because he drinks beer.

July the choirs sing
and the church bells ring.

August is really hot
Mum gives me cold drinks a lot.

September I go to school
and makes my chef cool.

October is Hallowe'en
witches and ghosts can be seen.

November hey it's bonfire night
what a marvellous sight.

December Christmas trees go up
and everyone gets a pup.

Steven Bonner (7)
St Mary's RC Primary School

MONTHS OF THE YEAR

January is snowing,
Then all the stars are glowing.

February brings the frost,
And lots of children get lost.

In March the snow melts,
And people wear big belts.

April showers plants can grow
And a lot of people do not know.

In May lambs are being born
And some people mow the lawn.

In June it is time to play,
Some people go on holiday.

July is the holiday,
And we make stuff with clay.

August it is time to play,
I see my friends on holiday.

September is that time of year
Now the harvest time is near!

October is Hallowe'en
Lots of ghosts can be seen.

November is bonfire night,
And the sky is very alight.

In December stars are glowing,
And people stop mowing.

Amy Capelo (8)
St Mary's RC Primary School

The Months Of The Year

January brings the snowflakes
Children stepping in the lakes.

February hear the church bells ring
Come and see the choir sing.

March hear the blackbirds sing,
Hooray today it's time for spring.

April flowers grow and spring,
All the animals play and sing.

May a new beginning,
Just the time to go out swimming.

Hot June is my mum's birthday,
It's summer time, let's go and play.

July, July school is out,
Hear the excited children shout.

August I go on holiday
What a pity I can't stay.

September is my birthday
I have friends over to stay.

October don't be afraid,
Lots of scary masks are made.

November is bonfire night,
What a wonderful sight.

December it's Christmas time
See the lights sparkle and shine.

Claudia Ruffini (8)
St Mary's RC Primary School

MONTHS OF THE YEAR

January makes the snow,
Then the strong winds start to blow.

February flowers coming out
Spring's around the corner, without a doubt.

In March bees buzz, birds sing,
Spring is such a wonderful thing.

In April animals run around,
On the ground there are nuts to be found.

May time the grass turns green,
In Miss Plunket's house there are cards to be seen.

June's here no time to play,
Pack your bags, we're going on holiday.

In July time flies by,
Mum's in the kitchen making plum pie.

August time summer's nearly over,
But Jack Brady's still going fishing in Dover.

September time, back to school,
I can't wait to go swimming in the pool.

October's here so beware
You might get a fright or a shock or a scare.

November's here it's my birthday,
I have a party of friends to stay.

In December there's fog and mist,
Time to write your Christmas list.

Lucy Molloy (8)
St Mary's RC Primary School

Jibbejabby

'Twas centac and the twiry tones
Did grille and gyme in the cape;
All lantg were the hicochores
And the toke liths lunape.

Beware jibbejab, my son!
The feet that crush, the claws that kill!
Beware the cranla bird and flun
The cunning waper-ill!

Gabriella Lewin (9)
St Mary's RC Primary School

School

S is for school where we learn
C is for computer work
H is for history it tells you about the past
O is for Oxford, who makes our text books
O is for obey which we have to do
L is for learning, which we do in class.

Dominic Alexander (9)
St Mary's RC Primary School

The Fork Song

Neither arms nor legs have I
But I have hair on my head.
And I have food, food, food.

Shaun Henry (10)
St Mary's RC Primary School

Dogs

Dogs are really cuddly and soft,
Most of all I like cocker spaniels.
Most of the time dogs re-landscape your garden,
I like it when you get in the door
And they are really happy to see you.

I really wish I could have one,
But I'm never there to feed it.
My mum's usually at home, she could feed it.
I would always walk it and teach it tricks.

I would love it so much
Hopefully it will love me too.
I would name it Max,
And its nickname would be Jumpy.

Ryan Bleach (9)
St Mary's RC Primary School

'Twas Creepy

'Twas creepy and the hairy fleas
Did squeak and demolish in the bathroom;
All beautiful were the maneating plants
And the indestructible mice sneezed.

Beware the ant, my son!
The legs that kick, the arms that punch.
Beware the spider and web.
The beautiful rattle snake.

Kiera O'Reilly (10)
St Mary's RC Primary School

The Puppy Song

Neither sight nor hearing have I
But I hop on my legs
And I have
Fur, fur, fur!

Neither fins nor scales have I
But I crawl on my paws,
And I have
Fur, fur, fur!

Neither big teeth nor small tail have I
But I sprint on my claws
And I have
Fur, fur, fur!

Michael Reilly (9)
St Mary's RC Primary School

Jiggerocky

'Twas spooky and the hunchbacked lizards
Did thrash and mash in the city;
All gungy were the dandelions
And the creepy eels fuzzed.

Beware the kasrock my son!
The teeth that crunch the horns that bash!
Beware the munjy fox and shun
The furious washron.

James Dalton (10)
St Mary's RC Primary School

BABIES

When my brother was a baby
He sucked his thumb,
Now he's quite smart
But then he was dumb!

My mum said he was hungry
But if you want to see,
Someone who was hungry,
You should have seen me!

Michael Bridges (9)
St Mary's RC Primary School

THE POPPIES OF WORLD WAR ONE

The poppies of World War One.
The battle was not at all fun.
Mothers were crying,
The soldiers were dying,
And children were calling for Mum.

Frederic Wise (9)
St Mary's RC Primary School

AUTUMN LEAVES

Autumn days when the sun is shining,
And leaves falling off the trees.
Red and golden crunchy leaves,
Children playing in the leaves.
Tossing, kicking, jumping, having fun.

George White (7)
St Mary's RC Primary School

Jibberish

'Twas brimy and the tonely grons
Did stim and slymak in the momp;
All crimey were the mimercoos
And the mar mak makomped.

Beware the Hammerwick, my son!
The jaws that crush, the claws that clutch!
Beware the Bli Bli bird and shun
The furious fagliament.

Frederic Wise (9)
St Mary's RC Primary School

Winter

W is for wind
I is for ice
N is for nice
T is for tears
E is for explore
R is for rain.

Nathan Registe (8)
St Mary's RC Primary School

The Spider Song

Neither arms nor wings have I
But I wiggle on my tummy
And I have
Fangs, fangs, fangs!

Michael Gymer (9)
St Mary's RC Primary School

Baby

Babies are cuddly
Babies are small
I wrote this for babies all.

B is for babies that like their Mummy.
A is for adorable ones that like their dummy.
B is for babies that like their Daddy.
Y is for you that will be grown up.

Grace Gerety (9)
St Mary's RC Primary School

Autumn

Brown leaves fall to the ground,
Brown conkers that I found.
Animals store food to keep
They are soon to sleep.
It is not so bright with less light
I need my jumper for the cold.
Autumn is here I am told!

Mark Golden (8)
St Mary's RC Primary School

Autumn

Autumn days
Until now it has been summer
The days are getting shorter
Underfoot are lots of leaves
More leaves are red
Now it is nearly Christmas.

Ashleagh Williams (8)
St Mary's RC Primary School

THE SEASONS

Spring the animals are out playing about.

Summer puts on a show
And all the places you must go.

Autumn leaves fall off the trees
Animals are hiding under piles of leaves.

Winter rains no sun again,
Up umbrellas down goes the rain.

Laura Blanks (7)
St Mary's RC Primary School

AUTUMN

A corns fall down
U nderneath the
T rees squirrels
U ncover
M eals of
N uts.

Robert Gissane (7)
St Mary's RC Primary School

AUTUMN

Autumn days are here again.
When the day gets short and the evening gets long.
The leaves turn brown and the conkers fall down.
The flowers die and the wind and the rain comes,
Howling once more.

Amy Wybrant (7)
St Mary's RC Primary School

VISITORS

Very friendly and kind
Is caring, loving and giving.
So nice and helpful and happy,
Is a helpful person.
The kindest one you know,
On your birthday they come round,
Ready to listen to what you're saying,
So we love them and they love us.

Laura McDowall (8)
St Mary's RC Primary School

AUTUMN

When the leaves are falling
Scattering colours of red and gold.
Night begins early, as the wind blows cold.
Looking out through the window,
Safe and warm inside,
Close the curtains
Autumn has arrived.

Stephanie Lawson (8)
St Mary's RC Primary School

LIGHTNING

It bangs and zig-zags
And flashes and crashes
And rushes and smashes.
It's a big thing.

James Maddock (6)
St Mary's RC Primary School

Autumn Days

All the leaves fall off the trees,
Typical there are no bumblebees.
Upset the sun's not shining,
Mad the heat's not climbing.
Daddy's cold every day,
And we're so far away from May.
All the flowers begin to die,
I know winter's coming so I think I'll cry.

Bradley Murphy (8)
St Mary's RC Primary School

Autumn

A utumn days, silver frost
U nusual coloured leaves
T ough frosted rings on moss
U nbelievable coloured trees
M ornings cold with frosted streets
N ight that's filled with stars!

Anne Walkin (8)
St Mary's RC Primary School

Autumn

A s the autumn days will pass,
U ntil the winter days will start.
T rees illuminate the splendour of autumn,
U sually when the leaves go golden,
M agical autumn is the best,
N ights are longer, days are colder.

Daria Ruffini (8)
St Mary's RC Primary School

Autumn

Autumn is the time when the leaves
Turn red, yellow, orange and brown,
And fall off the trees.
Autumn is the time to go walking in the forest
And crunch the leaves with your feet.
Autumn is the time when squirrels bury their nuts
And boys and girls go collecting conkers to play with.
Autumn is the time when all the trees and animals start
To get ready to go to sleep for the long winter.

Stefan Ruffini (7)
St Mary's RC Primary School

Autumn Poem

Our holidays were over,
It was time to go back to school.
Mornings were golden
Leaves were falling.
It was time to say happy birthday
To my daddy and brother,
The Harvest Festival was here,
Food was shared.

Catherine Dalton (8)
St Mary's RC Primary School

Snow

It's cold and white and frosty
And sprinkles and tinkles
And then quiet.

Thomas Killoran (6)
St Mary's RC Primary School

AUTUMN

Autumn is wonderful
Autumn is fun
You pick up conkers and you run.
Autumn is great, you are really happy
When you put on your wellies
And go climbing up trees and get conkers,
Then you go in and count your conkers.

Luke Bramley (8)
St Mary's RC Primary School

AUTUMN POEM

Autumn is when the leaves fall,
Upon the trees the wind blows.
Toys stay in for the wintertime
Umbrellas everywhere.
Misty as we go to school,
November 5th is bonfire night.

Tom Richardson (8)
St Mary's RC Primary School

AUTUMN

Autumn is when the leaves turn gold,
Autumn is when the weather's cold.
Autumn is when the animals fold,
Autumn is when the people stay inside,
Autumn is when animals hide,
Autumn is my birthday pride.

Jake Mara (8)
St Mary's RC Primary School

THE MONTHS OF THE YEAR

January has snowflakes,
Sit down and eat a cake.

February brings the snow,
and it makes my fingers glow.

March I go out and play in the snow,
And I tie a bow.

April I watch the flowers grow
And I go into my house and sew.

May brings the fluffy lambs,
And we see little dams.

June is my fun day,
I go out to play.

July school is out,
And we can hear boys and girls shout.

August is the time of year,
Go into the pub and drink some beer.

September is the time of year,
When we play with a deer.

October is Hallowe'en
We get into a team.

November brings shivering cold,
And makes us feel old.

December is the time of year,
And we see everything dear.

Laura Clarke (7)
St Mary's RC Primary School

The Fish Song

Neither speech nor arms have I
But I swim on my belly
And I have
Scales, scales, scales!

Megan Flannery (10)
St Mary's RC Primary School

The Frog Song

Neither arms nor fingers have I
But I hop on my belly
And I have
Slime, slime, slime!

Robert Blanks (10)
St Mary's RC Primary School

Charlie

Charlie was sad he hated his home,
He went to Berlin, Paris and Rome.
Charlie was very sad
'I hope I find one soon,'
'I've got it, I'll live on the moon!'
Charlie went away on a magical scooter
The tissues left behind was by him blowing his hooter.
Poor Charlie never came down,
On everyone's faces there were frowns.
Then Charlie jumped out from space,
Smack! Poor Charlie landed on his face!

Samuel Diss (9)
St Saviour's Primary School

My Teacher Shouts All Day

My teacher is old he has no hair,
He moans and groans like a grizzly bear.
All he does is sit in his chair
Then he shouts all day.

My teacher's strict we're in at play,
But not one word did we say.
He said we all get in the way
Then he shouts all day.

My teacher is dumb he drinks his tea,
And then for no reason shouts at me.
Just because he lost his keys
He shouted all day.

My teacher's dumb he's very fat,
He also has a tabby cat.
He tends to be a nutty bat
Because he shouts all day.

My teacher's tall, he's very sad,
But for me it isn't so bad.
Now he won't get so mad
And shout and shout all day.

Callie Moffat (10)
St Saviour's Primary School

Big Brothers

My big brothers are a pain in the neck,
They love to eat everything especially eggs.
They love to have their own sleepover,
When I'm not there,
See my brothers - now they don't care!

My big brothers like wearing hats,
But don't like guinea pigs because they think
they're rats.

So support me now and vote them out,
Otherwise they'll beat you without a doubt.

Chloe Leak (10)
St Saviour's Primary School

FRIENDS

My name is Sarah
I've got a friend called Jade.
All she really says to me
Is 'Why don't you go away?'
I sit next to Keris
And all we do is fight.
I sit next to Chris
And all he does is write.
My friends are very silly
But still they are fun
But Peter is the best
Because he helps me with my sums.

But sometimes I wish
They would go away
Because all they do is moan
Nearly every day.
But if I was to lose them I'll know
I'll feel lonely
Because it will be me
I myself Sarah only.

Sarah McDonald (10)
St Saviour's Primary School

My Big Sister

My big sister is horrible and mean
She's got ten boyfriends I haven't even seen.
She goes out late,
And brings back mates.
'Please Mum let them stay'
Then Mum says 'OK.'
It's just not fair
She just don't care.

One day she hit me round the head,
But I got in trouble instead.

It's time
For a crime
To be done
To someone.

Jade Smith (10)
St Saviour's Primary School

My Family

My sister's annoying,
My mum always moans,
My dad is so grumpy,
I feel like they're all mean clones.
My nan is so funny,
My aunt has lots of money.
My cousin is a DJ,
My uncle's nickname is PJ,
And that is the end of that.

Darren Paveling (10)
St Saviour's Primary School

Old Lady

There was an old lady,
Who looked very nice
She had a fast car
With some furry dice.

The very next day I saw her again,
She had a jelly with a flag on the end,
She went to the moon on a big fat spoon,
And brought down a big baboon.

The very next day I saw her again
She looked really sad and lonely.
A man went up to her and kissed her on the cheek,
She felt so embarrassed she stared at her feet.

He bought her some flowers,
And they got married,
And now all she does is moan.

Charlotte Eldridge (10)
St Saviour's Primary School

School Teachers

Teachers are dim,
Sometimes fools,
I even wonder why
We have them at school.
They talk all day non-stop
Sometimes they make my head blow off.
I sit and pray
For the end of the day
And hope I can watch the telly.

Keris Ratford (10)
St Saviour's Primary School

The Trip On A Pan

Once there was a man,
Who went surfing on a pan.
He went twenty five thousand miles
And then saw a little man.
He went straight over to him,
And told him to jump in.

They went a little further
And saw someone doing a murder.
They went straight over to him,
And told him to jump in.

They went on a little more
And saw a flying fish.
Flying in the sky and singing a lullaby.
They went straight over to him,
And told him to jump in.

They went on a little more
When a leak sprung in the floor
They fell into the lake
And along came a giant snake.
They swam and swam
But the snake got them!
Damn.

Chris Rowe (10)
St Saviour's Primary School

Food And Drink

All food is nice,
Like custard or rice.
When food goes crunch
I'll want a big bunch.

Flat drinks are old,
When they are cold,
And when tea is hot
I'll drink alot.

Charlie Lunn (10)
Wellington Primary School

ALIENS

Our world has been invaded by aliens
We need this madness to stop,
Not to be poisoned by any kind,
We've even called the cops.

Pack our bags
We need to go,
On our way, out of this land,
Without crumbled toes.

People screaming,
With terrible fear,
This nightmare
Is turning into a scare.

I've made an alien as my friend,
He has such slimy, green skin.
Disgusting looks with eight eyes,
And a nasty, stupid grin.

He likes to eat,
Filthy frogs,
Slippery fish with humans' intestine,
And old, smelly socks.

Antoinette Okoiye (10)
Wellington Primary School

Snow

I'm sitting by the window,
Watching the stars fall from the sky.
Each snowflake has only a short life,
Before it hits the frozen ground.

The snow that's fallen,
Looks like sprinkled icing sugar,
The green tufts sprouting through,
Look like the bristles of a broom.

My mind begins to wander,
Thinking what life would be like,
If we were surrounded by snow,
Both day and night.

It would look so pretty,
But oh so cold!
Hats and gloves and scarves,
Wellingtons, duffle coats and red noses.

The snowflakes drift down from a greying sky,
And they sizzle into the ground,
The snowflakes . . .
Are no longer around.

Kirsty Addae (10)
Wellington Primary School

School

I hate maths and science too,
But I like English and I like you.
Teachers are boring, so is school
But I think computers are cool.

PE is much more fun
Especially in the sun,
You can play duck, duck, goose,
But you won't see a moose.

Georgina Belverstone (9)
Wellington Primary School

ELEPHANT

There once was an elephant from Earth
Who liked eating plenty of dirt.
So then one day he went out to play,
But everyone laughed at his scarf.
He waved his trunk and stamped his feet,
Then jumped up and down on the spot.
It threw mud at the others,
And they told their mothers.
Then they came out
But then they shouted.
So he ran back home in a huff
Crying and crying he goes.
He waits for a pizza
Then has his dinner.
But had mud pudding for dessert.
Before he went to bed
He had a drink for the night.
He went to bed at eight o'clock
Then woke up at seven.
He walked around till half past ten.
Then he played with his hen.

Kimberley Ogborn (10)
Wellington Primary School

SPACE

Space, space, outer space,
It really will put a smile on your face.
Neil Armstrong allowed us to see,
The ultimate space odyssey.
Soon we will be able to go,
To Mars, Neptune or even Pluto.
We will try to avoid major space crashes,
And forget all the cosmic bashes.
Space, space it's so amazing,
Until that time we'll just keep gazing.

It's the year 2099,
Way past Neil Armstrong's time.
We discovered Planet X,
It was found by a man called Lex.
Next year we will be able to travel there,
And maybe even set up a fair.
We all want to see more,
Like Pluto's core.
We found it all, nothing to see,
In the ultimate space odyssey.

Yousef Shantir (11)
Wellington Primary School

SCHOOL

I like PE and English too,
But I hate maths and I hate you.
Teachers are boring so is school,
I like computers I think they're cool.

Playtime is much better,
But only when it's wetter,
'Cause then you can do skids,
But there's so many kids.

Jessica Gilbert (9)
Wellington Primary School

WARFARE

Upon the hills,
The battle fills.
The space around the Alps,
And on a mountain,
A colossal fountain,
Of bullets fills the air.

There was a flood
A flood of blood.
Flowing like a river,
And in a field,
The battle yields,
To the sound of a screaming boy.

There amongst the dead,
A bright red poppy showed its head.
On that field of battle,
Then a few thousand more,
What a glorious sight we saw,
And we never fought again.

James Page (11)
Wellington Primary School

I Love Music

I love music,
It's so cool,
I even take my Walkman in the swimming pool.
I love music in the morning,
I love music in the night,
I love music, I know I'm right.

I love music,
Everywhere I go,
It's booming in my ear,
On the sunny pier.
I love music in the morning,
I love music in the night.
I cuddle up with my radio, really tight.

Music here, music there, music's in the air.
We move to the beat,
We jump off our seat,
Music's better than going to the fair.

Luka Wells (11)
Wellington Primary School

Hair

Hair, hair, hair,
It is everywhere,
It is greatly special,
Because people give it care.

Hair, hair, hair,
Flying through the air.
When you're really hurrying,
It can sometimes be a scare.

Hair, hair, hair,
There's never a spare,
It sticks to your head,
So you can't grasp some off to share.

Hair, hair, hair,
It is everywhere.
It is greatly special,
Because people give it care.

Sam Jenkins (11)
Wellington Primary School

WINTER

Look out the window at the trees,
Look at the deadly leaves.
Winter is here,
The worst time of year,
The flowers were red but now they're dead.
Winter is a disaster.

The wind is blowing,
The snow is flowing.
The flames are burning,
People are turning,
To go into their house.

Go away leave us alone,
We are even cold in our home.
Go far yes go away,
You are stopping the kids play.

Yes it worked, you are gone,
Spring is here, come and sing along.

Nikki Lewis (11)
Wellington Primary School

The Book Fair Rush

Books stacked up all over the place,
The children decide to have a race,
The book fair commences at 1 o'clock
Now it's time for the doors to unlock.

Rush begins and people arrive,
People all start to dive.
Horror, adventure and joke books too,
One about a cow that goes Moo!

Little kids leap up and down,
Books collapse and people drown.
Books are grabbed and everyone runs,
Screaming at the top of their lungs.

'We've got some books! Without paying!'
The bookseller begins wailing.
'I haven't made any money yet,
And my forehead is covered in sweat!'

The fair is over in an hour,
And the seller begins to feel sour.
She packs up the books on the floor,
Before stomping out the door.

Stephanie Oliver (10)
Wellington Primary School

Without You

Without you, I'm like
a piece of paper without writing,
I'm like a playground with no children,
or a dog without an owner.

Without you, I'm like
A cupboard without food.
I'm like a computer without a keyboard,
or a Christmas without presents.

Sophie Whitfield (9)
Wellington Primary School

FOOTBALL

Crowds coming through the door
And even some sneaked in poor.
Some losers on the pitch
People falling in the ditch.
The pitch is big, wide and long,
Tottenham sing their almighty song.
It's pouring down with rain,
With one player in pain.
Injured souls
Some of the best goals.
Volcano ashes in the air,
Fireworks shooting everywhere.

Aaron Mitchell (9)
Wellington Primary School

THE CAT

The big white fluffy cat
Comes running down the stairs
Scrambling through the cupboards for food
Then he's staring at his shining white milk.
He trembles with fear
He starts dreaming of milk.

Lucy Bartlett (10)
Wellington Primary School

My Alien

My alien is green and tall and
Keeps on bashing into the wall.

My alien is round and fat
Keeps on putting on my hat.

My alien loves the park
And he is afraid of the dark.

My alien has lots of legs
And he eats the pegs.

My alien has to leave
Because he has got the fleas
Leaving green slime behind.

Ben Salmon (10)
Wellington Primary School

The Lonely Dog

There was a lonely dog,
He was walking in the fog.
It was a scary sight
As he got into a fight.
Then he carried on walking,
And then he tried talking.
But all he could do was bark
So he went to the park
And walked around in the fog.
That was the poem of the lonely dog.

Kieran Bishop (10)
Wellington Primary School

School War

There was a school war in a field,
Many people were sadly killed.
If you wondered 'What was the score?'
Here is a special guided tour.
Children ten and teachers none.
The headteacher died, it was no fun.

One teacher survived, it was a she.
Her name will live on in life to me.
The leader of the tribe was only ten,
So he killed that teacher, we won! But then . . .
Out of the blue from nowhere at all,
The Queen popped out and announced a ball.
She said to us in a splendid voice,
To choose a partner of our choice.
The children were making a terrible din,
'Oh no!' the teachers still could win!
They all ran off to find existence,
All they found was dust and distance.

Megan Faal (11)
Wellington Primary School

School

I hate maths,
I like PE and English too.
Science is alright,
History is too.
School is boring,
The teachers say that we don't listen,
But I bet we do.

Karly Lantieri (10)
Wellington Primary School

SCHOOL BOY

Once there was a little boy,
Who loved his Action Man toy.
He had teeth like a rabbit,
This boy really had a bad habit.
He picked his nose,
And bit his toes,
He had big blue eyes,
Yum he loved apple pies.
He always used to suck his thumb,
And had a very round tum.
This boy had a lizard tongue,
He only had one lung.
The boy had really smelly feet,
His best friend whose name was Pete,
Said 'Ah that's my boy.'

Rebecca White (11)
Wellington Primary School

SNOWMAN

S weating snowman in the sun,
N ever going anywhere,
O nly stares at the children
W ishing they would care.
M any have passed him
A nd wondered if they should stay.
N o one ever did though, so he just melted away.

Ellena Whitehead (9)
Wellington Primary School

SCHOOL

I remember when I was at school,
They treated me like I was a fool.
Punished me for trying to act cool,
Sat me in a classroom facing the wall.
Others had a laugh, but no fun for me,
I had maths when they had PE.
Practise for my GCSE
I was told the rest were better than me.
In English everyone got C,
Not me they gave me a G.
Sent to school on every birthday,
I had detention every Friday.
I had to work at lunch and play,
My mum had to come in to have her say.
'This is out of order,
My kid's the best at playing the recorder.'

Dwight Gayle (11)
Wellington Primary School

SHARKS!

The monsters of the deep
They will give you the creeps.
The little beady eyes make sure you don't escape.

They'll rip your skin apart,
And will make you into a tart.
Their massive sharp teeth,
You'll wish you weren't made of meat.
Their teeth are sharp,
But definitely doesn't sound like a harp.
Have you guessed I think you'll find it's a *shark!*

Francesca Calabrese (9)
Wellington Primary School

The Swimming Pool

To begin, just jumping in,
Second diving stop, belly flop.
Now you're older go third stop.
Splash, Pop
Now you're at the highest ever,
Try diving that's really clever.

Then we started races,
At very fast paces.
The swimming pool is cool
We're at the deep end now on the floats.
The floats have little picture goats on them.

Bye! We're going home now,
See ya later pal.

Chloe Bartlett (10)
Wellington Primary School

Niagara Falls

The flushing water of the falls
I was running around with all the seagulls.
The trustful American Falls
Thunder splash of the Niagara Falls.
Lightning speed of the ever fast water.
Old men, young men surfing over board,
And some just ignored.
The people on the boat were getting bored.
The boat began to sink,
'Goodbye Niagara' People would scream.

Nick Lustig (10)
Wellington Primary School

Dragon

There is a dragon in my garden,
He's breathing fire at me.
The sharp flames scorch my back.

There's a dragon in my garden,
Flicking its heavy green tail at me.
I'm swooped off my feet into the air,
And I fall to the ground with a 'thump!'

There's a dragon in my garden,
Holding me in his hands,
To take me to his lair,
In his lair he's cooking vegetables,
He finally picks me up with his enormous hands.

There's a dragon in his lair,
Cooking me for tea.
In a few minutes there'll only be bones left,
There's a dragon in his lair with a full tummy.

Joel Coppeard (10)
Wellington Primary School

Without You

Without you I'm like a gymnast without a beam,
a school without books,
a road with no cars.

I'm like a person without a friend,
a dolphin without water,
an ocean with no fish.

Hara Odesseos (9)
Wellington Primary School

FOOTBALL CRAZY

Once there was a boy called Ray
He loved football, he played every day.
But when he was on the field one week,
His team began a winning streak.
One match later
They didn't play any greater,
But are still on top of the league.

He went back to school,
Then at break, he played again.
He got tackled and complained
But then it started to rain.
He went inside, talked all day,
Wanting to get out and play.

Max Richards (10)
Wellington Primary School

THE ALIEN

An alien from outer space once came to town
It came out of its UFO.
With a big crown
And said 'I have come to invade the Earth.'

People ran so far,
As fast as they could
Some fainted,
Near walls that had been painted.

Some jumped into the ocean,
In slow motion.
And then the alien went
Straight back to outer space.

Tariq Patel (9)
Wellington Primary School

WARFARE

'Mum guess what we did today?
We locked all of the teachers away.
They taught us well, but are now in the dark,
They're in the manhole, in the park.

We had tables they had pens,
We bounced them like footballs then,
We gave them detention, kept them in,
Then we made a massive *din!*

Next we dressed them up like pigs,
It was really fun!'
'Time to do your homework dear,
And tidy your bedroom.'
'Mum!'

Rebecca Milnes (11)
Wellington Primary School

GAP, WHAT IS IT?

Gap, it's the place to be at,
Gap, it's the place where I never nap,
Gap, it's not a wonderland,
Gap, it's full of 'no' colour,
Gap, it's the best,
Gap, it's a monster's dream,
Gap, it's a weird thing,
Gap, it's a hole in the ground,
Gap, it's never been found,
Gap, it's not my home town.

Kayley-Ann Culling (10)
Wellington Primary School

The Wondrous Boy

As he wanders through the land,
The wondrous boy looks and stands.
He looks at everything he sees,
Even plants that look like these.
In a wonderful glistening way.

He finds a bird coloured black and white,
In the darkness of the night.
He stands and watches everything he sees,
Even the Queen bumblebee.
In a wonderful, glistening way.

He likes to sit upon the trees,
Saying birds come to me.
He watches birds sing and play,
In the sunny time of May.
In a wonderful, glistening way.

Laura Foster (11)
Wellington Primary School

The Girl Called Ellena

There once was a girl called Ellena
Who wished that her name was Ella
But she was a wrecker, so they named her Rebecca
And that's when the large sofa fell on her.

Her mum and dad were sad
But her friends and her teachers were glad.
For she was so bad, you might even mention mad,
So now we all call her *Die*anna.

Laura Clavey (9)
Wellington Primary School

Time Oh Time

Time is consuming, minute by minute, day by day.
Is it necessary to ignore the world, the war and the poor?
My life has time to pay attention to see those hurt,
Not to spend time in detention.
Everyone should take notice of their lives
And not sit oblivious to what goes on outside.

On and on people rush in, out and all around.
Have a little time to relax and sit down.

There are people who spend their time and days free.
In the building people work and work
And in their minds they go berserk.
Me I spend time with my friends,
It seems like our fun never ends.
End of the day had so much fun
Then I go home and hug my mum!

Adam Ayres (11)
Wellington Primary School

Monsters

I see a dragon through my window.
I see a monster under my bed.
I see a dinosaur doing a jigsaw.
I see monsters in my head.
I see a dragon making some stew.
I see a dinosaur pointing at me and you.
I see me and you cooking in the stew.
I don't see me and you.
I see bones.

Stephanie Gioia (9)
Wellington Primary School

A Girls' Night Out

C'mon everybody slap some lipstick on your face,
Make your hair sparkle like a shining star,
Ride around in your flashy car.

C'mon everybody sparkle and shine,
C'mon everybody we're losing lots of time,
We'll put some make-up on we can't forget that,
A snazzy suit and maybe a hat.

We'll clip some earrings on,
And don't forget the heels.
And we can't forget the flashy car,
We'll be riding on wheels.

C'mon everybody sparkle and shine,
C'mon everybody we're losing lots of time,
We'll put some make-up on, we can't forget that,
A snazzy suit and maybe a hat.

Lucy Higginson (10)
Wellington Primary School

Monster

My monster lives with me
On my wooden floor
Near my red settee
Stupid little monster
Turning around and around
Everything he knocks down
Ready to go back home.

Hollie Moss (9)
Wellington Primary School

Alton Towers

As my heart trembles and shakes,
As I wait and wait and wait,
And when I finally get there,
It's like a gigantic fair.

All the rides are bigger than me,
If you go there you will see.
Alton Towers is really great,
It's more bigger than a summer fete.

I thought Corkscrew was wicked,
But Hex is better.

Risha Parmar (9)
Wellington Primary School

Rabbits

Rabbits can run around,
Rabbits have sturdy fur,
Rabbits can be tamed,
But only if they listen to you.
Rabbits never growl,
Rabbits never bite,
Rabbits can be kings,
Or queens.
Rabbits can tell you if they need water or food,
But they're delightful as pets.

Pritpal Amrit (10)
Wellington Primary School

Football

I am excited that Man United are playing Arsenal today
But when we're losing,
We just keep oozing our way to victory.

Beckham takes a free kick
In it goes what a kick!
Ryan Giggs running down the pitch
Stops to pass, got a stitch.
How they're gonna win I don't know?
They think it's all over, it is now.
Man U won five nil, Man U have some skill.
Man U put on a show
No one dares have a go.

Bradley McVeigh (11)
Wellington Primary School

Food

Food is delicious,
when it's nutritious.
Food is good,
when it should.

We all need drink,
or we won't think.
When I munch,
I also crunch.

Hot dogs are nice,
unlike burnt rice.
When you eat properly,
you should eat broccoli.

Nicky Love (9)
Wellington Primary School

My Exotic Garden

I had an exotic garden
I shared it with Uncle Marlon.
It had trees and flowers
We sat there for hours
Eating a chocolate muffin.

Mum said she wanted my garden
'No you can't, I beg your pardon.'
'What shall I say to Uncle Marlon?'

When winter came it wasn't fun
My toes were cold and my hands were numb.

Then summer came I couldn't wait,
Let's play about and jump and shout
In my lovely exotic garden.

Terri Green (11)
Wellington Primary School

Frost

Frost, frost everywhere,
Frost is in the air,
Frost lies on the ground,
You're sure to slip,
It's an icy trip.

Grit, grit on the floor,
So you can walk to your door.
Grit, grit dissolves the ice,
No more slipping, tripping, hooray! hooray!
Maybe summer will arrive in a day.

Charlotte Toumazos (11)
Wellington Primary School

WITHOUT YOU!

Without you I'm like a tree with no leaves,
I'm a road with no cars,
or a school with no pupils
and a city with no buildings.

Without you I'm like a book with no words,
I'm like the sun with no shine
like a musician with no instruments,
the moon with no craters.

Without you I'm a failure,
without you I'm no good,
you're my very best friend,
because you always understood.

Rebecca Sherwin (10)
Wellington Primary School

FIRE, FIRE

Sharp hot fire fills the room,
The boys all run around as can be.
Sharp hot fire burns their skin,
The fire flickers and flickers.
The room is quiet now,
It glimmers and flutters and flickers.

The room glitters as the fire burns,
It twinkles and twinkles
As we sit and stare.
Then suddenly the room is starless
The coal tumbles away, away
And away.

Laura Goode (11)
Wellington Primary School

Germany Vs England In The World Cup Final

The crowd were cheering and dancing around,
With the England flag flying high.
A person from the crowd shouted
Come on Owen score a goal.
At half time the score was 1-1
The second half started with all the England fans shouting
Come on England
Germany made a great run
But what a save by David Seaman,
And what a boot
And what a header by Heskey
Goal Latzio, and the final score was
2-1
To England
And England won the World Cup.

Charley Cohen (9)
Wellington Primary School

Are Man U The Best?

Man United think they're cool
David Beckham what a fool.
David Beckham's filthy rich,
Then he comes and scorches the pitch.
Andy Cole tries to score a goal,
But what a miss it hits the pole!
Sheringham is so tall
But now he's got the blooming ball.
Andy Cole thinks he's a scorer,
But I think he's rather a borer.

Daniel Somner (9)
Wellington Primary School

YORKSHIRE TERRIER

Getting late, time for bed,
I'll tuck you in by the sharp hot fire.
No barking now you little terrier
Close your eyes, no more to see.
We'll see you in the morning.

Wake up now, time to eat,
For breakfast you've got meat.
The redness warmth of the fire,
Fills the house with sultry, warm air.
Snuggle up with me, let your food go down.

Go on now, doze away
Ease your head on my comfy lap.
I'll keep you warm till the end of the day,
Till you wake, I'll still be here
Don't fret, I won't go anywhere.

Ella Coulson (10)
Wellington Primary School

HIGHBURY

A lot of fans travelling by trains,
When they get there, they're a pain.
All the players getting rich,
While we're sitting there watching the pitch.
I bought a can of 7 Up,
And drank it slowly from a cup.
Then the players went mad,
And the referee was sad.

Stephen Hodges (8)
Wellington Primary School

My Only Fish

I'm going to meet my mum
But something happened.
I had a little fish
My cat ate in his dish.
I hate my cat but I just want
My little fish back.

I'm now still waiting
I know he's dead
But I just want my
Little fish back.

I'm now gone
I've been sick.

Lucy Reynolds (11)
Whittingham Community Primary School

Open Door

Beyond the black door,
Total darkness,
Black like coffee
Black like my boots
Never light
No way out
Total darkness
I'm scared.

Timothy Akinbogun (9)
Whittingham Community Primary School

THE GREEN AND CLEAN ALIEN

I'm an alien from outer space
I like my leg, but not my face
I use my shop to tour the universe
It's so safe I don't need a nurse.

When I went to the sun
I had loads of fun
Before I left they gave me a bun.

After the sun I went to Mars
Where all the aliens hang cans and jars
On the back of their floating cars.

Then I went to Neptune
Where they got out a fork and spoon
And said they were going to eat me soon
So I escaped in their cold air balloon.

On the way to Mercury
I got in a bit of a fury
So they gave me some hot curry.

So then I went to the moon
And met a looney toon
When I left they said see you soon.

Then I went to Earth
Where I played football on some astroturf.

When I left Earth to go to Saturn
I got a very bad sunburn.

So I got a doctor and went to Venus
And we had to discuss
Who to take on their dangerous bus
So they took one of us.

So I went to Jupiter
Where they cover themselves with fur
They were very weird
Because they all had a beard.

I was so pleased to go to Pluto
To see a load of Kabuto
They were all chasing after me
So I had to flee.

When I went to Uranus
They made me sing a chorus
That made a stampede of Taurus
Chased me into the deep blue sea
And before I drowned I said no more of me.

Ryan Cooper (10)
Whittingham Community Primary School

On A Planet

On a planet
On a planet,
Zooming!
On the bike
On a planet
On a planet
Zooming.
In my car
On a planet,
On a planet
Zooming!

Jessica Read (10)
Whittingham Community Primary School

LISTEN

Listen,
Can you hear the children crying because they are upset?

Listen,
Can you hear the children singing in the playground?

Listen,
Can you hear the children clapping as they play a game?

Listen,
Can you hear the bell ringing at the end of play?

Christina Lee (9)
Whittingham Community Primary School

THE SECRET BOX

I found my box in a haunted dark beach that no one goes to.
Its lid is carved from garbage that is smelly.
Its hinges are made of dinosaurs bone and hedgehogs spikes.
If you press your ears to the sides of the box,
You will hear devils killing and monsters screaming.
My box contains the secret of Hell.

Chika Ndubuokwu (9)
Whittingham Community Primary School

SAFARI ADVENTURE

I am going on safari to see creatures
To explore on a motorbike
I can get to places quicker
And to see creatures that are alive.

I go to safari to have fun
And to learn about what animals do
The creatures are friendly and they are nice
I'll bring one home for you.

Kyle Clarke (10)
Whittingham Community Primary School

MY SECRET BOX

I found my box in a pearl from an oyster's mouth.
Its sides are made of spiders legs.
The lid is carved from gold and silver from the sun and moon.
Its hinges are made from the mane of a lion.
If you put your ear to my box you can hear vicious
Splashes of the sea.
My box contains the secret of what happened to all the witches.

Matthew Griffin (10)
Whittingham Community Primary School

THE SECRET BOX

I found my box floating on the glittering ocean.
Its sides, were made from snakes' scaly skin.
Its hinges were made from a blue whale's gut.
Its lid was made from mouthwatering chocolate.
If you press your ear to it you can hear my
Secrets of the ocean.
My box contains evil sphinx and emerald cloaks
From the warriors.

Tomris Ozaktanlar (9)
Whittingham Community Primary School

THE JOURNEY

The journey is long
The ship is turning turning
We went past Hong Kong
The waves are as silent as a tree
The sailors have lost my keys
I feel sick so give me a kick
Twisters are coming *Help!*

Sean Lecomte (10)
Whittingham Community Primary School

MY SECRET BOX

I found my box trapped in the middle of a crocodile's mouth.
Its sides are made from cats' whiskers.
Its lid was carved from a leopard's skin.
Its hinges are made of caterpillars' bones.
If you press your ear to it you will hear the sound
Of the splashing waves hitting on the rocks.

Shikira Gordon (9)
Whittingham Community Primary School

THE SECRET BOX

I found my box hidden beneath the graveyard.
Its sides are made of thick dried rusty dinosaur bones
Its lid is carved from rough lizard tongues.
Its hinges are made of dried up bits of meat.
If you press your ears you would hear the sound of dinosaurs roaring.
My box contains the secret of death.

Amy Ellison (9)
Whittingham Community Primary School

SNOWBOARDING

Snowboarding is like a trip through the North Pole
Never knowing what's going on.
On my way there I would say I just can't wait.
When I get there I'm jumping up and down.
Beginning to get cold and starting to frown.
OK then, I will say, I will do this even if I'll be sick.
As I get going I will say, 'Oh please Lord, don't let me die today.'
Racing up
Diving back down
Ice everywhere
No grass to be found
Gong down, down, down, down.

Michaela Scott (10)
Whittingham Community Primary School

THE SECRET BOX

I found my box under my dad's voice,
When he was singing me a song.
Its sides are made of the wind and the breeze
That he blows in the sky.
Its lid is made from sweets and lovely flowers.
Its hinges are made of lots of lovely bright sunlight.
If you press your ears to the side of the box
You will hear songs from outer space.
My box contains the wind of power and love.

Shayna Lawson (9)
Whittingham Community Primary School

LISTEN

Listen
Can you hear the teacher dismissing the class?
Listen
Can you hear the children shouting, 'Hooray'?
Listen
Can you hear the adults screaming at the children?
Listen
Can you hear everybody teasing you, 'Bo ho ho'?
Listen
Can you hear the children crying because the football hit them?
Listen
Can you hear yourself talk, but not now because the bell has struck!

Gemma Stone (9)
Whittingham Community Primary School

ADVENTURE IN THE JUNGLE

A dventure in the jungle.
D angerous as can be.
V aluable objects you can find,
E xpert you will be.
N ature will pass you Wow!
T winkle up the sun hiding behind the trees.
U nusual things may pass you.
R ecord what you find or see.
E xpert you will be
S tay the night and return tomorrow.

Nadine Gore (10)
Whittingham Community Primary School

THE MAGICAL JOURNEY

Once I went on a magical journey,
With plant so straight and incredibly curly.
It was a magical, beautiful and colourful land,
With red velvet carpet which I thought was grand.
I lived in a castle with a flag on top,
And saw cute rabbits that would wriggle and hop.
One day I saw a lilac tree
And saw a nightingale singing sweetly.
I tried to catch it but it flew away,
Then I decided to go away.
I went to the castle to have a cup of tea,
And then for a swim in the deep blue sea.
Then I decided to go back home again,
Then my voyage came to an end.

Zoyah Imran (11)
Whittingham Community Primary School

DRIVING IN A CAR

Driving makes me sick
Running smoke all over the place,
Indicators flashing
Vengaboys on the radio,
I'm going to be sick
Noise so loud
Goi! I've been sick.

Heather Roffey (10)
Whittingham Community Primary School

Flying On My Broom

He-he
I'm a witch
Flying round on my broom
To hurt innocent people.

Ha-ha
You can't stop me
With one flick of a finger
You'll be just like me.

Hey-hey
Go away.
I'm wicked and bad
So don't mess with me.

Tina Mensah (10)
Whittingham Community Primary School

Listen

Listen, can you hear children
Kicking the football over the fence?
Listen, can you hear the dog,
Barking on the other side of the fence?
Listen, can you hear people screaming
At each other?
Listen, can you hear children whispering
To their friends?
Listen, can you hear the ball bounce on the ground?

Joe Dunn (9)
Whittingham Community Primary School

My Time Travel Adventure

Going on a time travel,
To see what I can see.
Going on a time travel
To relive history!

I'm going to see Jesus
In his little manger;
I'm going to see Jesus
While he was in danger.

Jesus was in danger
He's known since he was born.
Jesus Christ was crucified,
That day was Friday morn.

Came home from my time travel,
I've seen all I could see.
Came home from my time travel
I've relived history!

Natalia Robinson (11)
Whittingham Community Primary School

My Secret Box

I found my box
In a treasure chest on a pirate's ship.
Its sides are made from smooth, stinging, scorpion skin.
Its lid is carved from an alien's sticky, wet, rough tongue.
Its hinges are from human bones.
If you press your ear to the sides of the box
You will hear the loud furious roar of a dinosaur.
My box contains
Fire breath from a dragon's mouth.

Tyree Cater (10)
Whittingham Community Primary School

My Secret Box

I found my box
In the centre of a dragon heart
It was bright like a diamond.
Its sides are made of
Eagles' wings that are as beautiful as gold.
Its lid is carved from badgers' claws
That are so sharp they will cut your arm.
Its hinges are carved from the dark cave of wonder.
If you press your ears to the sides of the box
You will hear bones crunching.
My box contains
The heat from the biggest volcano.

Jerrell Darbo (9)
Whittingham Community Primary School

Fish

Fish,
as gold as a ring,
that swims slowly through the Earth,
in a blanket of happiness.
Fish,
like summer rain,
lips like red roses,
eyes like the seas,
bringer of love.

Rebecca Wyatt (9)
Whittingham Community Primary School

TROTTING ALONG ON MY HORSE TO THE BEACH

I was trotting along on my horse to the beach
Trotting, trotting, trotting along.
Sun was beaming rides were gleaming
Trotting, trotting, trotting along.
Water and waves splashing near
Trotting, trotting, trotting along.
Fun and laughter all around me
Trotting, trotting, trotting along.
Swimming, relaxing all day long
Trotting, trotting, trotting along.

Stephanie Lashley (11)
Whittingham Community Primary School

ON MY RATTLE SNAKE

I was moving through the silky sand on my rattlesnake
When suddenly,
I saw a pig holding up a rake.
I was moving through the splashy water on my rattlesnake
When suddenly,
I saw a cloud smiling at my face.
I was flying through the night sky on my rattlesnake,
When suddenly,
I was no longer on my rattlesnake
Aaahh!

Sahariyea Siddique (11)
Whittingham Community Primary School

AROUND THE WORLD

I am a little fishy under the sea,
When a whale submarine swallowed me.
It took me to Paris, it took me to York,
It took me to Torquay it took me to Cork.

Now I've found out why it kidnapped me,
It wanted to show how big the place could be.
I'm just a little fish look at me,
I'm just a little fish in the sea.

The whale submarine has talked to me,
It loves little fishes for company.
When we went to London we went for tea,
I love tea when it's just for me.

Then we went to the Bermuda Triangle,
I wanted to get a marvellous view.
Then there was a great tornado in the sea,
And then all my bones were left in the sea.

Nathan Onojaife (10)
Whittingham Community Primary School

THE SECRET BOX

I found my box under the ocean in a sunken ship,
Its sides are made of red roses and buttercups,
Its lid is carved from an ancient golden tooth,
Its hinges are made of gold and silver pearls,
If you press your ears to the sides of the box
You can hear music playing softly,
My box contains a fairy's wand and the key to
Everything you could imagine.

Samantha Harvey (9)
Whittingham Community Primary School